A STEP BY STEP PATH TO EASE OVERTHINKING AND CREATE INNER PEACE

MANIISHAA RAJPUT

Clever Fox®
PUBLISHING
Chennai • Bangalore

CLEVER FOX PUBLISHING
Chennai, India

Published by CLEVER FOX PUBLISHING 2026

ISBN: 978-93-7500-191-1

PREFACE

Every journey begins quietly - not with fireworks, but with a faint stirring beneath the noise of ordinary life. This book was born from that stillness. It is for the moments when life feels full yet hollow, when success feels rehearsed, and when something deep within whispers for honesty, for breath, for space to feel again.

A step by step path to ease overthinking and create inner peace is not a manual of quick healing or rigid steps. It is a gentle unfolding - a map written in soft lines and pauses, guiding you inward and then outward again. Each chapter invites reflection, presence, and compassion. The movement is circular, not linear; you will revisit emotions, memories, and truths you thought you had already met. This is not repetition, but refinement - the quiet art of becoming whole.

The pages ahead blend insight and intimacy. They speak of masks and exhaustion, of breaking and rebuilding, of returning to the self that has always waited beneath the noise.

Along the way, you will find gentle techniques to rest the mind and soothe the body - ways to meet stress, anxiety, and restlessness with awareness rather than resistance.

This book asks only for your presence. Read it slowly, as you would a letter written just for you. Let its rhythm breathe with yours.

You may not find grand answers here, but you will find doorways - into stillness, into softness, into the unguarded spaces where healing begins.

At its heart, this work is a conversation between strength and gentleness, between what you've carried and what you're ready to release. It is a reminder that love endures, that softness is courage, and that every return - however quiet - is a beginning.

Welcome home, to the self that never truly left.

ABOUT THE BOOK

This book is a quiet journey into the landscapes of the self - an exploration of what it means to heal, to unlearn, and to come home to one's inner truth. It is not a story of perfection or quick transformation, but of gentle remembering. Through reflective storytelling and poetic insight, it invites readers to slow down, listen within, and rediscover the strength that lives beneath softness.

Each chapter moves like a breath - expanding and returning - guiding you through the many layers of becoming: the masks we wear, the breaking that clarifies, the silence that teaches, and the tenderness that rebuilds. The journey is not linear; it spirals through emotion, awareness, and renewal, reminding us that growth often comes disguised as return.

Blending psychology, mindfulness, and lyrical wisdom, the book offers both depth and practicality. Alongside its reflections, you'll find subtle techniques for calming the mind and easing the nervous system - gentle ways to meet stress, anxiety, and uncertainty with presence rather than resistance. These practices are not instructions, but invitations: to breathe deeper, to soften your inner dialogue, and to find steadiness in awareness.

At its heart, this book is an ode to balance - between courage and compassion, strength and surrender, solitude and connection. It celebrates the art of gentle living in a world that often forgets to pause. Each page carries the reminder that healing is not the end of struggle but the beginning of understanding; that love, once awakened, does not fade - it transforms.

This is a companion for anyone seeking stillness amidst motion, clarity amidst confusion, and the quiet courage to be real. It does not promise escape from life, but a deeper way of walking through it - alive, aware, and whole.

ABOUT THE AUTHOR

Born in a small town in North Maharashtra, Maniishaa Rajput transformed a humble beginning into a lifelong pursuit of learning, empathy, and inspiration. With over twenty-eight years of experience as an educator, subject expert, and master trainer, she has guided students and teachers across rural and urban India, nurturing not only minds but hearts.

A scholar of English Literature and Education, Rajput has qualified the NTA NET and MHSET examinations and earned PGCTE and PGDTE credentials from the English and Foreign Languages University, Hyderabad. She is presently pursuing a PhD in English Literature and has completed the Goethe Institute A2 Level in German-proof that curiosity, for her, is a lifelong companion.

What began as classroom insight evolved into a calling: to help others face inner storms of fear, trauma, and anxiety with compassion and clarity. Her writing blends academic depth with emotional warmth, offering readers a space to reflect, restore, and rediscover their quiet strength.

Beyond her work, she remains an avid reader of self-development literature and a believer in kindness as the highest form of intelligence. Through every page she writes, Rajput invites readers to learn, heal, and live with gentle courage.

ACKNOWLEDGEMENTS

This book was not written in isolation; it was shaped by the quiet strength of many hearts who walked beside me - often unseen, yet always felt. To each of them, I owe gratitude that words can only begin to touch.

To those who shared their stories, their silences, and their raw truths - thank you. Your courage to speak, to feel, and to begin again gave this book its pulse. Every chapter carries a reflection of the lives that opened themselves to honesty and healing.

My deepest appreciation to my husband and my kids, whose gentle eyes saw what I meant even when I could not yet find the words. Your sensitivity preserved the soul of this work while guiding it into clarity. To the clever fox publishing team, for believing in the quiet power of introspection and allowing this book to breathe in its natural rhythm - thank you for your trust.

To my mentors and teachers, who reminded me that gentleness is not weakness but wisdom in motion - your lessons echo through every line. To my friends and family, who gave me patience during the long silences of writing, and love without demand - your presence became my ground.

To every reader who chooses to enter these pages, I offer deep respect. May you find a mirror here, a resting place, and a spark of remembrance. Healing, after all, is not solitary; it moves in spirals between souls, weaving one person's courage into another's awakening.

And finally, to the quiet - to the spaces between thoughts, where truth waits without pressure and light returns on its own. It was in that stillness that this book was born, and it is there I leave my gratitude - whole, wordless, and real.

CONTENTS

PART I

THE HIDING

CHAPTER 1

THE MASKS WE LEARN TO WEAR

From the earliest breaths of life, we are offered scripts to inhabit. At home, we slip into the role of the obedient child who wins affection with compliance, the caring sibling who puts others first, or the ambitious achiever who carries the pride of the family.

In school, these scripts expand, the diligent student who never forgets homework, the adaptable friend who blends seamlessly with the group, the one praised for fitting in rather than standing apart.

Later, as adults, the repertoire multiplies: in the workplace, we become reliable professionals who measure words carefully and polish gestures to match the occasion. In society, we adjust again, shaping fragments of ourselves to meet expectations, soothe others, and earn applause.

Roles, in themselves, are not enemies. They are the scaffolding of human connection, allowing families to function, communities to cooperate, and institutions to endure. Yet with every role comes an adjustment.

One part of the self is softened to avoid offense, another is hidden because it feels too raw, another edited so it sounds more agreeable. Slowly, the mask takes shape.

At first, it feels like performance. Over time, it fuses with the skin. What began as choice turns into reflex.

Beneath all these performances lies another presence: the unfiltered self. It is the part that longs to laugh at the wrong moment, to say no without explanation, to speak truth even if it unsettles the room. This hidden self is not rebellious, nor is it fragile. It is simply authentic.

Yet it waits quietly, because the world so often rewards the mask more than the face.

We wear these masks not out of cowardice but out of longing, the longing to belong. Belonging is among the deepest of human needs, and so we learn to bend, to cover, to conform. For a time, it works.

Acceptance is won. Safety is secured. But beneath the surface, the authentic voice grows quieter. What once rang vibrant now murmurs faintly, pressing against layers of practiced performance.

The tension between roles and authenticity rarely erupts loudly. It whispers. Relief when finally, alone. The sigh that escapes after a day of holding it together.

The tiredness that no sleep seems to cure. These signals remind us: the hidden self is alive, waiting to be remembered.

Approval Culture and the Birth of False Selves

As we move deeper into life, this tendency to hide is magnified by the culture of approval surrounding us.

Approval is no longer the smile of a parent or the praise of a teacher; it becomes woven into every fiber of modern living. A child's worth is measured in grades.

Popularity is displayed through likes and shares.

Professional value is tied to applause after presentations or recognition on performance charts. Even love is at times confused with compliance, as though harmony requires unbroken agreement.

Within such conditions, the mask grows heavier. Adjustments that once seemed harmless become habitual. We smile when weary, convinced it is polite.

We agree when uncertain, believing it avoids conflict. We offer help when empty, imagining it proves kindness. Each act, in isolation, is small.

Yet repeated endlessly, these actions form grooves. The grooves carve patterns. And patterns, over years, harden into identity.

Slowly, the line between genuine and performed self-blurs. Was that smile born of joy or duty? Did I agree because I believed or because I feared judgment?

What began as conscious effort becomes unconscious reflex.

The cost arrives quietly but insistently. The first cost is disconnection, from feelings, from instincts, from inner truth, as we learn to check the reaction of others before checking the voice within.

The second cost is restlessness, a low unease that lingers even when life appears perfect on paper.

The third is anxiety, the constant hum of worry that one day the mask will slip, that someone will glimpse the unpolished self we have hidden.

These costs do not always crash in suddenly.

They collect slowly, like dust gathering in corners: subtle fatigue that no rest lifts, joy shrinking from moments that should sparkle, life moving with efficiency yet hollow at its core. Success is achieved but not savoured, belonging is secured but feels strangely empty.

And yet, beneath every mask, the authentic self remains. It shows itself in bursts, unguarded laughter, unplanned tears, courage that rises without rehearsal.

These glimpses remind us: the hidden self is not lost. It waits. It endures. It presses gently against the surface, asking to be remembered.

Invitation Forward

Noticing these signals is not failure. It is the first thread of awareness, the beginning of return. Each time we ask,

Who am I beneath these roles? What truth have I silenced in my search for approval? we loosen the hold of the mask.

The journey toward authenticity does not begin with rebellion but with remembrance. It begins with small choices: laughter allowed to ring freely, honesty chosen in a simple exchange, refusal spoken without apology.

Each choice becomes a crack in the mask, an opening toward freedom. And in those cracks, light enters, pointing us toward what lies ahead.

The Price of Constant Acting

Every performance has a price, and the roles we rehearse daily are no exception. When the curtain never falls, when the applause becomes the only measure of worth, the self begins to tire. At first, the performance feels natural, a smile offered at work, patience extended in family, charm displayed in public.

But when these gestures are repeated without pause, without the balance of honesty, they transform from expressions into obligations.

What once connected us to others now quietly distances us from ourselves.

Think of the workplace, where a professional might wear the mask of unfailing competence. Mistakes are swallowed, doubts hidden, emotions pressed into silence.

The performance secures trust, perhaps even promotion, but the inner self begins to shrink. Or consider the family gathering, where laughter is polished and stories rehearsed to avoid tension. The warmth looks genuine, but behind the scenes sits a fatigue born of constant acting.

These examples show how masks infiltrate even ordinary spaces, until performance feels like the only safe language.

The cost of always performing is subtle but profound. It seeps into ordinary moments: the conversation that feels scripted rather than spontaneous, the laugh that rings hollow, the endless calculation of how to appear acceptable.

The body feels the weight first, shoulders tense, breath shortens, rest feels incomplete.

The mind follows, restless even in stillness. The heart, too, begins to ache, not from dramatic wounds but from the quiet erosion of authenticity. To live as a constant performance is to live with an invisible drain, one that empties energy faster than it can be restored.

The Quiet Exhaustion of Pretending

This exhaustion is not always visible to others. From the outside, the performer may look accomplished, admired, even envied. But inside, the unspoken fatigue gathers.

It is the fatigue of always managing impressions, of monitoring every gesture, of guarding every word. It is the kind of tiredness that no holiday or weekend can repair. Because the exhaustion is not physical, it is existential.

It comes from the distance between the face we wear and the self we silence.

Pretending, over time, becomes heavy. Not because the mask itself is unbearable, but because the self beneath longs to breathe. Suppression demands constant effort.

To deny truth is to hold a door closed against a force that insists on opening. And so, the body, the mind, and the spirit spend their strength in maintaining a false calm, a pleasing façade, a harmony that costs too much.

Cultural rituals often reveal this strain. Take the festival where everyone dresses in bright colours, dances, and sings.

Beneath the music, some carry sorrow, anxiety, or exhaustion, but feel compelled to mask it for fear of spoiling the collective joy.

Or picture the friend group where one member always plays the joker, hiding his loneliness behind laughter. The performance entertains, but the unspoken weariness deepens. These scenes remind us that the exhaustion of pretending is not rare; it is a silent companion for many.

This fatigue erodes more than energy.

It diminishes creativity, dulls relationships, and numbs the ability to feel deeply. When everything is filtered through performance, spontaneity vanishes.

Even simple pleasures, a walk, a meal, a quiet conversation, become tasks on a stage. The cost is not measured in hours but in the slow erosion of joy.

First Cracks When Authenticity Peeks Through

Yet the story of masks is not only about cost. Cracks inevitably appear. These cracks are not failures; they are beginnings.

A sudden burst of laughter that breaks through restraint. A refusal spoken unexpectedly, even softly, but with clarity.

Tears that arrive unplanned, carrying more honesty than words. Moments like these are the quiet rebellions of the authentic self. They remind us that beneath the layers, something real endures.

These cracks may unsettle us at first. We fear being seen without the mask, worry that others will not understand, wonder whether approval will be withdrawn.

But if we look closer, we notice something else: in these unguarded moments, connection deepens.

People respond not only to the mask, but to the glimpse of truth that shines through. Authenticity, even in fragments, has a magnetism that performance cannot replicate.

A teacher who admits uncertainty in front of students may discover respect rather than judgment. A parent who apologizes instead of pretending to be infallible may create intimacy rather than distance.

A leader who acknowledges vulnerability may inspire more loyalty than a leader who pretends to be unshakable. These examples show that cracks are not signs of weakness; they are bridges toward connection.

The journey forward is not about discarding every role or stripping away every mask. Roles will always exist, and masks sometimes serve as protection.

But it is about balance, allowing the authentic self to breathe through the roles, ensuring that the mask does not become the whole face.

To recognize the cracks as invitations rather than threats is the first step toward wholeness.

These small cracks, once noticed, begin to guide us inward. From recognizing roles and false selves, we now enter deeper territories, where masks start to slip, and the mirror reflects not only what we display, but also what we conceal.

Each crack in the performance is not an ending, but an opening toward the next layers of self-discovery.

CHAPTER 2

THE WEIGHT OF YES

There are words we learn to speak almost before thought has formed. "Yes" is one of them. It slips from the tongue quickly, as if rehearsed, often before the heart has had time to consult with itself.

This reflex is not born from weakness, but from a history of belonging-our first lessons in love, approval, and connection.

From childhood, "yes" carries rewards. We nod when asked to finish our vegetables, and a smile greets us. We agree to share our toys, and approval warms the air.

We learn, slowly and subtly, that harmony flows more easily when we yield, when we align, when we accept. Families, schools, and communities often celebrate the child who complies, who adapts, who bends.

The reflex of "yes" is planted early, watered by praise, and reinforced until it feels less like a choice and more like the rhythm of life itself.

When Yes Becomes Identity

Over time, this rhythm seeps into our identity. To say "yes" becomes not only an answer but a form of self-definition. It tells others,

I am helpful. I am agreeable. I am safe to love.

The word carries the promise of connection. And so, we say it again and again, often without pausing to ask if the promise costs more than it gives.

But every reflex, however noble its origin, carries shadows. The "yes" spoken too often, too quickly, begins to blur the edges of selfhood.

It is not that generosity is wrong, or that openness is unwise. Rather, when "yes" comes before awareness, we begin to lose sight of the true intention behind our choices.

We forget the sacred difference between the wholehearted yes that affirms our values and the automatic yes that erodes them.

Society and Safety

Society deepens this conditioning. In many societies, politeness is equated with obedience.

To refuse is to risk disapproval, to seem unkind, uncooperative, or even selfish.

At work, "yes" may promise advancement, the mark of someone dependable. In friendships, it may appear as loyalty. In love, as sacrifice.

The reward is belonging, and the cost is often unseen: a slow drift away from authenticity.

This reflex thrives because belonging is among our deepest human needs. We yearn to be part of something larger, to be held in circles of acceptance. "Yes" appears to be the easiest bridge into that circle.

Yet if every bridge is crossed without pause, we may one day arrive at destinations never chosen by our own soul.

Psychologically, the reflex of "yes" is tied to our wiring for safety. To please others feels secure. To maintain harmony shields us from conflict. The nervous system relaxes in the moment of agreement, sparing us the discomfort of tension. But what soothes us briefly can unsettle us in the long run. A thousand small yeses, unexamined, can leave us carrying weights that were never ours to bear.

The Hidden Cost and the True Yes

There is a subtle exhaustion that grows from this habit-an inner weariness not always visible from the outside.

Life may appear smooth, relationships untroubled, work accomplished. Yet within, there is a quiet imbalance: the sense that decisions are no longer born from clarity but from compulsion.

Identity blurs in the repetition, as if the self has been painted over by the expectations of others. One day we wake and realize that while many are satisfied with us, we are not fully at ease with ourselves.

It is important to see this not as failure, but as inheritance. The reflex of "yes" is a story we carry, passed down through families and cultures that prized harmony and survival.

It is the story of keeping peace, of avoiding fracture, of being welcomed into the fold. To recognize it is to honor where it came from, even as we begin to ask if it still serves the life we long to live.

Each yes carries weight.

Too many, and we forget how light a true yes feels. The wholehearted yes is spacious-it affirms who we are, aligns with our values, and nourishes our energy.

The reflexive yes, by contrast, can feel heavy, like a garment borrowed from someone else's wardrobe. We wear it because it fits the occasion, not because it belongs to us.

The invitation is not to abandon generosity or to resist connection.

It is to bring awareness back to the act of agreeing. To notice, in the small pause before the word escapes, whether it springs from alignment or reflex.

That pause is where freedom lives. In that space, we rediscover the difference between being true to ourselves and merely being acceptable to others.

The reflex of yes is a beginning, not a sentence. It reveals our longing for connection, our instinct for survival, our capacity for care.

And yet, it also signals the places where choice has fallen asleep. To awaken it is to remember that saying yes is not thc only way to belong.

Sometimes, belonging deepens when we have the courage to speak otherwise.

The Quiet Price

There are moments when the word "no" rises naturally on the inside but never makes it past our lips. Instead, we soften it, reshape it, replace it with the more familiar "yes."

The silence around refusal is not born from lack of thought, but from a quiet pressure that stretches across cultures and generations. Saying no can feel like stepping into danger, while saying yes feels like stepping back into safety.

The difference is less about truth and more about the weight of expectation.

The guilt tied to refusal begins early. Children who say no too often may be labeled stubborn or difficult, while those who comply are praised as cooperative and kind.

Over time, this pattern becomes a script: agreement equals goodness, resistance equals fault. Even as adults, this script whispers through our choices. Declining an invitation feels like disappointing a friend. Refusing extra work feels like letting down a team.

Saying no to family feels like breaking a sacred bond. The word itself takes on an emotional charge far heavier than its two letters suggest.

The Hidden Cost of Compliance

This heaviness explains why so many of us hesitate. A refusal is not just a word; it carries imagined consequences.

We picture disapproval flickering across a loved one's face, judgment slipping into a colleague's eyes, or conflict rising in the air.

These unspoken fears, though rarely named, hold great power. They guide our decisions in subtle ways, nudging us toward compliance even when our heart longs for space.

Authenticity becomes the silent casualty. Every time we say yes against our inner truth, a small fracture appears between who we are and what we present.

One or two fractures might go unnoticed, but over years they weave into a quiet dissonance.

Life on the surface looks smooth, but inside there is a gap, a distance from the self that longs to live with clarity.

The cost of this distance is felt not only within us but also around us. Stress rises when we overload ourselves with obligations we did not freely choose.

Anxiety lingers as we replay interactions, wondering if we should have spoken differently. Burnout creeps in when the rhythm of overextension becomes routine. Emotional fatigue settles when we realize that much of our energy is spent on sustaining appearances rather than living authentically.

This is not heaviness for its own sake, but a truth quietly lived by many.

The human spirit is not designed to live in constant performance. Each misplaced yes is a withdrawal from the self, a slow draining of vitality.

The irony is that we often intend these yeses as gifts-gifts of time, service, presence. Yet gifts offered against our truth rarely carry the fullness of joy.

They may be received politely, even gratefully, but the giver remains quietly diminished.

Ripples Beyond the Self

Relationships, too, bear the ripple of this pattern. A partner who constantly agrees may appear easy to live with, yet unspoken resentments accumulate.

A friend who never refuses may seem endlessly generous, yet beneath the surface, fatigue clouds genuine connection.

In workplaces, employees who cannot decline requests may be admired for dependability, yet their hidden exhaustion eventually affects creativity, morale, and trust.

Even families, bound by love, can become tangled when no one feels safe to speak honestly. The absence of "no" may preserve harmony in the moment, but over time it creates a distance far greater than any single refusal could.

The quiet price of misplaced yeses is not merely personal; it is collective.

When authenticity is suppressed, communities lose access to the diversity of voices and perspectives that make them strong.

When people give beyond their capacity, workplaces lose the brilliance that emerges only from rested, honest minds.

When boundaries are absent, families risk confusing compliance with love, when true love flourishes only where honesty can breathe.

And yet, this price is not paid in despair.

It is paid in small realizations, the moments when we recognize that our smiles feel practiced, our calendars overfilled, our energy thinner than it should be.

These recognitions are not punishments; they are signals. They remind us that life is asking for recalibration, that our choices want to return to balance.

Saying no, then, is not an act of rejection but an act of preservation-of energy, of authenticity, of relationship.

To recognize the quiet price is to begin loosening its hold. Each time we notice the reflex to agree, we create an opening to ask ourselves:

Does this yes serve connection, or does it serve only appearance? Does it honor who I am, or only who I am expected to be?

The answers to these questions do not arrive in thunder. They arrive gently, like light filtering through leaves.

They reveal that the cost of refusal was never as dangerous as we feared, and the price of automatic yes was greater than we imagined.

In seeing this, we step closer to a freedom that belongs not just to us, but to everyone touched by our choices.

The Courage of Boundaries

To many, the word "no" still carries the taste of rebellion. It feels sharp, as though it cuts the thread of harmony, as though it denies love.

Yet this is a misunderstanding handed down through generations. A true and mindful "no" is not an act of resistance but an act of respect-respect for one's own limits, and respect for the authenticity of the relationship in which it is spoken.

When we say no from clarity rather than fear, we honor both ourselves and the other.

To deny what we cannot truly give is to prevent false promises, to guard against the quiet erosion of trust. A yes offered against our truth may win temporary approval, but it leaves behind a subtle fracture.

A no offered from honesty may surprise, but it carries a strength that deepens connection. In this way, no becomes not a weapon but a gift.

Circles of Light

There is hidden courage in a healthy no. Courage not because it defies others, but because it requires us to stand in our own center. It is far easier to bend, to please, to comply.

It is far harder to risk disappointment, to allow another to see our boundary and still trust we are worthy of love. This is the bravery of authenticity:

The willingness to be fully known, even when our answer does not meet expectation.

Boundaries, then, are not barriers. They are circles of light drawn gently around us, defining the space where we can live with integrity.

Within those circles, our energy renews, our voice strengthens, and our giving becomes genuine. To set a boundary is not to push others away; it is to ensure that what we offer comes from fullness, not depletion. It is to say,

This is where I end and you begin, and both are sacred.

The protection boundaries provide is not merely practical, though they do shield us from exhaustion and overextension. They are also deeply psychological.

Boundaries preserve our sense of identity in a world that constantly asks for adjustment. They remind us that care must include the self, that love is most powerful when it flows from authenticity.

In this way, boundaries become instruments of growth: they create the conditions in which we can flourish without losing ourselves.

The Ripple Effect of Honesty

This flourishing ripples outward. In relationships, a clear boundary fosters trust.

Partners know where each other stands; friends learn that honesty is safe; families discover that love can include difference. In workplaces, boundaries encourage sustainable collaboration.

Colleagues respect each other's capacity, creating an environment where creativity can thrive without burnout.

In communities, boundaries honor diversity, allowing people to contribute their unique gifts without erasing their individuality.

It is tempting to imagine that constant agreement keeps bonds strong.

Trust deepens when words align with truth. We come to rely not on endless yeses, but on the knowledge that when a yes is given, it is real.

The authentic no does not weaken a relationship; it purifies it. It removes the fog of pretense, leaving behind clarity and strength.

This reframing shifts the entire meaning of refusal. No longer is it a wall that divides, but a doorway into genuine connection.

To say no is to choose honesty over appearance, courage over comfort, long-term trust over momentary ease. It is to say:

I value this relationship enough to bring my whole self into it.

Each time we practice this, the fear lessens. The first no may tremble on the tongue, but with time it grows steadier.

We realize that most bonds are not so fragile as to break over honesty.

In fact, many grow sturdier because of it. Even when others do not immediately understand, they often sense the integrity beneath our words.

And integrity, over time, inspires respect.

There is beauty in remembering that boundaries are not rigid lines but living spaces.

They shift as we grow, as seasons of life change, as our capacity expands or contracts. What remains constant is their purpose: to protect the conditions in which love, creativity, and joy can flourish.

They are less about exclusion and more about clarity-about letting others see where we stand so that what we share is real.

The courage of boundaries invites us into a new rhythm of yes and no. No longer automatic, no longer reflexive, each choice becomes intentional.

We say yes when our heart aligns, when our energy is present, when the offering is true. We say no when our spirit signals that giving would compromise our wholeness. In this rhythm, life feels lighter.

Our yes regains its brightness because it is no longer weighed down by pretense.

When no is honoured, yes regains its power. The two words, often seen as opposites, are in fact partners.

Together, they shape a language of authenticity.

Together, they draw the map of a life lived in balance.

And together, they remind us that freedom is not in endless compliance, but in the courage to choose with awareness.

CHAPTER 3

WHEN SAFETY BECOMES A BINDING

Love, in its purest form, is meant to liberate. It is the current that allows us to step into the world with courage, knowing we are held by invisible threads of belonging.

Yet there are moments when that same love begins to close in, weaving itself not into wings but into chains. The paradox of care is that it can both nurture and confine, depending on how it is expressed.

Often, control disguises itself as protection. A parent who insists their child never ventures beyond sightline does so not from malice but from fear.

A partner who checks every decision, every step, does so in the name of keeping the bond safe. Communities create rules to shield their members, and while these rules offer comfort, they sometimes stifle individuality. The arms meant to shield us can, at times, tighten into invisible chains.

The Quiet Cost of Overprotection

Overprotection rarely announces itself loudly. It arrives quietly, wrapped in the language of care. "I only want what's best for you."

"I worry about you." "I'm keeping you safe." These phrases are born of genuine affection, yet they sometimes carry an undertone of distrust-distrust in our ability to choose, to risk, to stumble, and to rise again.

Without meaning to, those who love us may place a ceiling over our growth, mistaking security for wholeness.

The psychological cost of such overprotection is subtle but profound. Confidence withers when choices are consistently made for us. Resilience weakens when every obstacle is removed before we can encounter it.

Creativity shrinks when our steps are measured against standards that are not our own. Slowly, the protected self begins to confuse safety with limitation, mistaking the absence of freedom for the presence of love.

Families are often the first stage where this dynamic unfolds. A child may be sheltered from disappointment so thoroughly that they never learn how to process failure.

Their achievements sparkle, yet behind the brilliance lies fragility. In adulthood, the memory of overprotection can linger as hesitation: the fear of making decisions, the constant search for external validation, the quiet unease of stepping outside familiar boundaries.

In partnerships, the same thread appears in different patterns.

A partner who constantly worries may cloak their concern in endearments, but the effect is similar-the other begins to feel watched rather than trusted.

Love becomes a lens of surveillance, one that narrows possibility instead of expanding it. What began as devotion can shift into dependence, not by intention but by the gradual erosion of autonomy.

Identity is shaped not by self-discovery but by inherited scripts. And while belonging offers comfort, it can also become a binding when difference is seen as danger.

None of this comes from cruelty. More often, it comes from fear-the fear of loss, the fear of vulnerability, the fear of the unknown. Love mixed with fear creates a paradox: it promises safety while quietly binding freedom.

It soothes in the moment but unsettles in the long arc of life. To be shielded too closely is to miss the chance to discover our own strength.

Trust as True Care

Yet it is possible to honor the love within this control while also naming its cost. The intention behind protection is noble: to keep harm away, to spare suffering, to preserve joy.

But intention does not erase impact.

When protection overreaches, it teaches us to equate love with restriction, as though to be cherished is to be confined. The gentle chains of love, though born from tenderness, leave marks on the spirit all the same.

The realization often comes in moments of contradiction. A child longs to climb higher, yet a parent's voice calls them down. An adult yearns to make a daring choice, yet hears echoes of "be careful" in their mind.

A community member desires to express a new thought, yet hesitates under the weight of tradition. These moments reveal the quiet tension between love and control, showing us that what protects can also prevent.

To see this dynamic clearly is not to reject love but to refine it. True love trusts.

True love allows space. True love understands that growth requires not only safety but also the risk of stepping beyond it. The arms that truly nurture are those that can hold and release in equal measure.

The gentle chains of love remind us that care is most powerful when it empowers. It is not the absence of risk that makes us strong, but the presence of trust. And when love remembers this, its embrace becomes not a binding but a circle-one that surrounds us with support yet leaves the horizon open for flight.

Fear in Disguise

Fear often dresses itself in the language of love. It speaks softly, assuring us that the restrictions it places are for our protection.

Parents speak of safety as they hover, partners frame limits as devotion, leaders shape rules as shields against uncertainty.

On the surface, these gestures seem harmless, even caring. Yet beneath them runs a current of fear-fear of risk, fear of change, fear of the unknown.

This fear does not always reveal itself directly. It wears the mask of concern.

A parent may say, "I can't bear to see you hurt," but what lies beneath is their own anxiety about letting go. A partner may insist, "I only want to keep you close," but beneath it is a fear of abandonment.

Communities or leaders may insist on conformity "for the common good," while quietly wrestling with fears of disruption or loss of control. The words sound protective, but the roots are entwined with fear.

When fear leads, the result is often dependency. Decisions are made for us rather than with us.

A child shielded too closely may grow into an adult unsure of their own judgment. A partner who is constantly directed may lose touch with their own preferences, relying instead on what keeps the peace.

Citizens within a tightly controlled community may forget how to imagine alternatives, mistaking obedience for harmony. Slowly, choice slips away, not because it was stolen, but because it was surrendered under the weight of love laced with fear.

The loss of autonomy unfolds quietly. It rarely arrives in dramatic gestures; rather, it appears in the small hesitations of daily life. The pause before making a decision, waiting for someone else's approval.

The silence when asked for an opinion, unsure if one's voice will be welcomed. The reluctance to step into the unfamiliar, because safety has been equated with staying small.

These subtle signs point to a deeper truth: autonomy withers when fear cloaked as care becomes the guiding force.

Toward Clarity and Freedom

The psychological costs of this dynamic are real, though often hidden.

Confidence falters when choices are not practiced. Self-trust diminishes when every step is guided by another. Anxiety grows as the world outside the protective circle begins to feel larger and more intimidating.

Identity blurs when the lines between our own desires and others' expectations become indistinct. The individual is still present, but their voice is muffled, their presence softened by constant accommodation.

It is important to remember that these consequences are rarely intended.

Most often, they are born of love-love that fears loss, love that seeks certainty, love that wishes to shield. Recognizing this removes blame and invites compassion. Those who overprotect are not villains; they are simply human beings navigating their own vulnerabilities.

At the same time, acknowledging intention does not erase impact. A binding built from care confines as surely as one built from control.

The path toward freedom begins with noticing these disguises. When we see how fear hides beneath care, we can begin to separate love from control, protection from limitation. Awareness does not demand rejection; it asks for clarity. It invites us to honor the love while loosening the fear.

To say: *I see your care, and I cherish it. But I also see the fear beneath it, and I choose not to let fear guide my life.*

This reframing transforms the dynamic. Instead of carrying forward patterns of dependency, we learn to step into partnership-with parents, partners, leaders, and even ourselves.

Decisions shift from being made for us to being made with us. Safety expands beyond restriction into trust. And autonomy, once muted, begins to find its voice again.

In this way, the recognition of fear disguised as care becomes not an accusation, but an opening.

It is the moment when we begin to remember that true care does not shrink us-it strengthens us. Love, when freed from fear, does not bind; it releases. And in that release, we rediscover the courage to live as our fullest selves.

Awakening from Comfort

There comes a moment, often quiet but unmistakable, when the comfort that once felt like shelter begins to feel like confinement.

The familiar patterns that once soothed us start to press against our skin like garments too small. What seemed like protection is suddenly revealed as limitation, and the very walls that promised safety now whisper of boundaries we have outgrown.

This recognition does not arrive with bitterness. It emerges gently, like light seeping through a crack in a closed room.

A student who has always been shielded from difficulty notices that their confidence falters when challenge finally appears. An adult, long accustomed to another's careful guidance, realizes their own voice feels faint, unused.

A partner senses that devotion has turned to dependency, and longs for breath, for space. These realizations are not betrayals of love-they are awakenings.

They signal the truth that comfort, if clung to too tightly, can suffocate the very growth it once intended to protect.

The Turning Point of Awareness

Awareness is the turning point. When we see the difference between nurture and confinement, safety and stagnation, we begin to reclaim our freedom. The binding, once mistaken for sanctuary, transforms into a mirror.

It reflects not only the love that built it, but also the fear that sustained it. In that reflection, we are invited to grow-not against love, but beyond fear.

Awareness does not erase what has been. It honors it. It says: *The care I received kept me alive, gave me stability, taught me belonging. And yet, for me to flourish, I must now step outside the limits of that care.*

In this way, the binding is not condemned; it becomes the ground from which courage rises. It shows us what we have outgrown and invites us toward new horizons.

Reframing comfort is central to this awakening. Comfort is not the enemy. We need it to rest, to heal, to feel held. But comfort was never meant to be permanent residence-it is meant to be a pause along the journey.

When comfort turns into confinement, it loses its nourishment. True comfort is dynamic: it nurtures without restraining, it shelters without silencing, it supports while still inviting movement.

Choosing spaces that nurture without confining requires both discernment and courage.

It means recognizing the difference between being protected and being prevented. A nurturing space says: *I trust you to try, even if you stumble.*

A confining space says: *I cannot risk your fall, so I will not let you climb.* In the first, love breathes with trust; in the second, love contracts with fear.

Trust as Expansion

The empowering message hidden in this realization is simple yet profound: true love trusts. It releases. It allows expansion. It believes in the resilience of the one it cherishes.

Parents who release their children into the world with faith give them wings stronger than any binding could offer.

Partners who trust each other's independence cultivate intimacy that is chosen, not imposed. Communities that honor individuality grow not weaker, but stronger, because they are enriched by diversity.

When love remembers to trust, its embrace becomes spacious. It no longer holds too tightly, fearing loss. Instead, it becomes a circle wide enough to contain both closeness and freedom.

Within that circle, growth feels safe, and exploration feels supported. The paradox resolves itself: safety and risk are no longer enemies, but companions.

For in the presence of trust, even risk carries a sense of belonging.

This awakening often unfolds gradually. A person begins to say yes to opportunities they once hesitated to take. They speak words that once felt unsafe to voice.

They step into unfamiliar territory with the quiet assurance that even if they falter, they will find their balance again. These are not acts of rebellion; they are acts of alignment.

They show that life, when lived fully, asks us to stretch beyond what once felt sufficient.

As we awaken from comfort, we carry with us gratitude for the protection that shaped us, but we no longer let it define us. We understand that safety was never meant to be the absence of challenge. Safety is the presence of trust-the trust that we are capable, the trust that we are resilient, the trust that love can endure even as we step into the unknown.

Safety is not the absence of risk-it is the presence of trust. And in that trust, we find both freedom and belonging, wings and roots, the courage to step out of the binding and into the vastness of our own becoming.

PART II

THE BREAKING

CHAPTER 4

THE MIRROR OF TRUTH

There are moments in life when the reflection looking back at us no longer feels familiar. We catch sight of ourselves-sometimes in the glass of a mirror, sometimes in the quiet of solitude, sometimes in the sharp honesty of another's words-and something shifts. The mask slips.

The practiced roles dissolve. For a fleeting instant, we glimpse the person who has always been waiting beneath the layers. The shock of this encounter can feel like both revelation and rupture.

For years, perhaps decades, we may have rehearsed an identity polished by expectation. We learned to smile when tired, to nod when uncertain, to keep moving even when our spirit begged for rest.

That polished self is not false-it carried us through, kept us connected, gave us belonging. Yet when the true self emerges, we realize how much of our life has been lived in costume. The recognition is startling, not because the authentic self is unworthy, but because it is raw.

It carries no script, no disguise, only the unedited truth.

Silence and Recognition

The first shock of meeting this self is the silence it brings. There are no words rehearsed, no gestures prepared.

It feels as though we are standing before a stranger who somehow knows us better than anyone else. The familiar rhythms of approval and performance fall away, leaving us face-to-face with the essence we had hidden.

It is not easy to meet this essence, because it does not flatter or disguise. It simply is.

In that moment, we may notice how distant we have drifted from what is most real.

Perhaps the reflection shows a fatigue we have long ignored, or a longing we have silenced, or a strength we have underestimated.

Perhaps it reveals joy that still flickers beneath the weight of responsibility, reminding us that we are more vibrant than we allow ourselves to appear. Whatever it shows, the impact is profound: a sudden awareness that beneath the life we present lies another life, equally present, waiting to be lived.

This awareness carries both discomfort and liberation. Discomfort, because it challenges the structures we have built-the roles, the masks, the expectations we have carried like armor. Liberation, because it reveals that we are more than those structures.

The shock is not only in the difference between the mask and the face; it is in the recognition that the face has never left us, that it has been patiently waiting, untouched by pretense.

An Invitation to Explore

Meeting this self can feel like standing at the edge of a vast landscape. At first, it is overwhelming. We do not know the terrain; it feels unfamiliar, even dangerous.

But as the eyes adjust, beauty begins to emerge. What once felt frightening becomes filled with possibility. The shock softens into curiosity, and curiosity becomes the invitation to explore.

The mirror of truth does not judge. It does not scold us for the years spent in disguise. Instead, it offers clarity.

It says: *This is who you are beneath it all. Will you have the courage to live from here?*

The question is not about abandoning the roles entirely, for roles are part of life. It is about loosening their grip so that the authentic self can breathe through them. It is about allowing the true voice to sing, even when the choir expects harmony.

This confrontation often arrives unexpectedly. It may come through loss, when the roles we depended on are stripped away. It may come through change, when new circumstances demand honesty.

It may come quietly, in the stillness of a morning when we see ourselves clearly for the first time in years. Regardless of how it arrives, the encounter marks a threshold. Once seen, the truth cannot be unseen.

The shock of confronting the real self is also a gift. It interrupts the cycle of automatic living and awakens us to choice. Suddenly, we are aware that the stories we tell about ourselves are not fixed. We can write them differently.

We can choose which roles to keep, which masks to lay down, which truths to embrace more fully. The encounter does not diminish us-it expands us.

And though the first glance may feel unsettling, the longer we remain in that gaze, the more familiar it becomes.

The stranger in the mirror begins to look less like an intruder and more like a friend. We realize that the authenticity we feared might isolate us is the very thing that can reconnect us-more deeply, more honestly-with those around us.

In this way, the mirror of truth is not only personal; it is relational. To meet ourselves honestly is to offer that honesty to the world.

The shock of confronting your real self is not the end of the story-it is the opening chapter of a deeper one.

It reminds us that life is not simply about perfecting the performance, but about remembering the essence beneath it.

And when we dare to meet that essence, we step into a freedom that is both humbling and profound: the freedom of being exactly who we are, without disguise, without apology, alive in truth.

The Shield of Denial

When the truth of who we are begins to rise to the surface, it rarely arrives to instant acceptance.

More often, it is met with resistance, a hesitation of the heart that whispers, *This cannot be me.*

Denial is not the absence of truth but the shield we instinctively raise when truth feels too vast, too raw, too disruptive to the life we have carefully arranged. Inner conflict is born from this tension: the pull between the comfort of the familiar mask and the call of the authentic self.

Denial takes many forms, most of them quiet and subtle. Sometimes it sounds like reason:

I am fine the way I am. Nothing needs to change.

Sometimes it cloaks itself in comparison: *Others have it worse. My struggles are not real.* At other times it wears the face of deflection: *It's just stress. It will pass.*

Each form serves a single purpose-to keep us within the boundaries of the known, to delay the uncertainty that comes with stepping into unedited truth.

This denial is not a weakness; it is a protective reflex. The psyche shields itself when it senses disruption, just as the body flinches when touched unexpectedly.

For many of us, identity has been shaped over years of performing, pleasing, and adjusting.

To suddenly glimpse the possibility of a different self is both thrilling and destabilizing. Denial steps in to soften the impact, to give us time to adjust to what we have seen.

The Tension Within

But beneath denial, conflict stirs. We sense the gap between the life we show and the life we long for. We go about our routines, yet somewhere within, questions rise. Why does success feel incomplete?

Why do moments of joy carry an aftertaste of restlessness? Why does silence feel louder than words? These questions create friction between the surface and the depth, between what we claim to be and what we quietly know we are.

Inner conflict can feel like standing at a crossroads with no clear sign. One path leads back to the roles that have brought belonging and approval, safe but constrained.

The other leads into the unknown of authenticity-open, expansive, yet without guarantees. The heart pulls in both directions, wanting the safety of the familiar and the freedom of the true. This tension is not failure. It is the natural landscape of awakening.

Psychologically, this conflict manifests as dissonance-a lack of harmony between inner truth and outer action.

It is the sigh that escapes after a day of smiling through fatigue, the hesitation before saying yes when we mean no, the quiet unrest in moments that should bring peace.

These experiences are not flaws; they are signals. They reveal that denial is thinning, and truth is pressing forward.

For some, this dissonance creates restlessness. Sleep feels shallow, conversations feel rehearsed, and accomplishments lose their savor.

For others, it shows up as hesitation-a difficulty in making decisions, an uncertainty about desires, a constant weighing of what others expect against what feels real. All of these are signs that the inner self is asking to be heard, even as denial tries to quiet the voice.

Thresholds of Growth

The beauty within this conflict is that it points toward growth. Denial delays truth, but it cannot erase it. The authentic self does not vanish; it waits.

And each wave of conflict brings us closer to recognition. The very discomfort we feel is evidence that we are awakening, that our spirit is no longer content to live in disguise. What seems like struggle is, in fact, movement.

To meet this conflict with compassion is essential. Too often we judge ourselves for not accepting truth instantly, for hesitating or resisting.

But awakening is not a single event-it is a process. Denial provides a buffer, and conflict provides momentum. Together, they prepare us for integration. They ensure that when we finally embrace our authentic self, we do so not with shock alone, but with readiness.

This part of the journey teaches us patience. It invites us to listen more deeply to the whispers beneath denial, to honor the questions that rise in the quiet.

Instead of rushing to resolve the tension, we learn to sit within it, to allow the conflict to clarify what matters most.

In doing so, we discover that denial and conflict are not obstacles, but thresholds. They are the spaces we pass through on the way to living more truthfully.

The mirror of truth, once glimpsed, will continue to call us back. Denial may delay our gaze, conflict may cloud our clarity, but both exist only because truth is already present.

The authentic self has stepped into the light, and though we may hesitate, the path forward is already opening.

Anxiety Born from Self-Avoidance

Anxiety often appears as a restless hum beneath the surface of daily life, an unease that seems to have no single source.

Yet beneath this hum lies a quiet truth: much of our anxiety grows from the effort of avoiding ourselves.

When we turn away from what is real within us-our feelings, our longings, our fears-we create a tension that no amount of distraction can dissolve. It is not the truth itself that unsettles us most, but the energy we spend resisting it.

Self-avoidance is rarely intentional. It slips into our routines in ways that seem harmless. We fill every pause with noise, every silence with activity.

We immerse ourselves in responsibilities, telling ourselves we are simply being productive. We scroll through endless images, watch stories that are not our own, immerse in the busyness of others' lives.

Each of these becomes a subtle way of turning away from the mirror within. For a time, this avoidance feels easier than facing what we carry. But beneath the surface, the untouched truths begin to press for attention.

The body often feels this tension before the mind names it.

A quickening heartbeat during moments of quiet, a tightening in the chest when we are alone, a restlessness that no achievement can soothe. These are not random disturbances; they are signals.

The self longs to be acknowledged, and when it is silenced, it speaks through the language of the body. Anxiety is often the voice of the self saying: *Look at me. Do not forget me. I am here.*

Avoidance and Its Paradox

The paradox is striking. We avoid ourselves to feel safe, yet the avoidance is what creates unease. We fear that facing our deeper truths will overwhelm us, yet the act of turning away is what multiplies the weight.

A feeling unacknowledged does not disappear; it waits, it gathers, it insists. The longer it is denied, the louder it becomes, until anxiety spreads like background static through every part of our lives.

This does not mean we have failed.

It means we are human. Self-avoidance is a strategy the psyche adopts when it feels unprepared for what lies within. It is a form of protection, a way to buy time.

The problem arises when avoidance becomes the default, when we mistake postponement for resolution.

Then, what began as a shield slowly transforms into a burden, carried day after day.

Consider the individual who buries grief beneath constant busyness. On the surface, their life looks full, even successful. But in the quiet moments, anxiety emerges-tightness in the body, shallow sleep, a persistent sense of unease.

The grief has not disappeared; it lingers, waiting to be acknowledged. The anxiety is not the enemy. It is the messenger. It is the reminder that wholeness cannot be built on avoidance.

Or think of the person who hides longing behind endless compromise, who silences desire to meet expectations.

They smile, they perform, they succeed-but within, anxiety whispers of the gap between what is lived and what is true. The unease is not punishment; it is signal. It calls them back to authenticity, reminding them that the self does not vanish simply because it has been ignored.

Turning Anxiety into a Guide

The path through this anxiety is not to suppress it, nor to fear it, but to listen. When we allow ourselves to pause, to feel, to name what we have been avoiding, something shifts.

The tension softens, not because the truth has changed, but because we have stopped resisting it. Even the smallest act of acknowledgment-writing in a journal, speaking a quiet confession, sitting with our emotions without judgment-can create relief.

In that moment, anxiety begins to loosen its grip, for its message has been heard.

Awareness transforms avoidance into invitation. Instead of fleeing the self, we begin to approach it with curiosity. What is this unease trying to show me?

What have I left unspoken? What part of me is asking to be remembered? These questions turn anxiety from a shadow into a guide. They remind us that the very feelings we resist contain the keys to our freedom.

This does not mean the journey is effortless. Facing ourselves can feel raw, unfamiliar, even intimidating.

But each step toward acknowledgment builds strength. Each moment of honesty teaches the nervous system that truth is not a threat but a path to peace.

Slowly, the body begins to relax, the mind clears, the heart steadies. What once felt unbearable becomes bearable, and what once felt frightening becomes a source of clarity.

The more we practice this, the more we realize that self-avoidance was never a solution; it was a delay. Anxiety born from avoidance is not a life sentence but a signal flare, guiding us back toward alignment.

When we learn to heed it, anxiety becomes less of a storm and more of a compass. It points us toward the places where attention is needed, where healing waits, where the authentic self is asking to step forward.

In this way, anxiety is reframed not as an enemy but as an ally-an imperfect but persistent reminder that we cannot outrun ourselves.

When we stop turning away, when we begin to meet ourselves with honesty, the restlessness quiets. The hum softens into stillness. And in that stillness, we discover not only relief but also the deeper truth: that peace comes not from avoidance, but from presence.

The Pain and Freedom of Honesty

Honesty is a threshold many approach with caution. It glimmers with promise, yet it also carries the weight of disruption. To speak or even admit the truth within ourselves can feel like tearing through fabric long held in place.

The roles we perform, the harmony we try to preserve, the expectations we strive to meet-all of these can feel threatened when honesty enters the room. And yet, without honesty, life remains dimmed, filtered through a veil that dulls both pain and joy.

The pain of honesty begins in its stripping away. It asks us to lay down the masks we have worn and to reveal what lies beneath.

To say aloud, *I am not as content as I appear. I am more fragile than you think. I long for something different than what I have been given.*

These admissions can feel piercing, not only because of what they reveal to others, but because of what they reveal to ourselves. Once spoken, they cannot be undone. They rearrange our perception of who we are.

This pain is not destructive; it is clarifying. Like light entering a dim room, it first blinds before it illuminates. We squint against it, uncomfortable with its brilliance, but soon we begin to see clearly.

The pain lies in the adjustment, the shift from shadow to clarity. It is the ache of muscles stretching after long stillness, necessary for movement but unsettling in its first pull.

Illusions and Renewal

Honesty also asks us to release illusions that have comforted us. Perhaps we have believed that approval was the same as love, that success guaranteed fulfillment, that silence equaled peace.

To admit otherwise is to dismantle the scaffolding we have leaned on for years. The fall of these illusions can sting.

Yet it also clears the ground for something sturdier to rise. Pain becomes the cost of renewal, the evidence that we are stepping away from false structures toward foundations that can truly hold.

At times, the pain of honesty comes not from what we admit to ourselves but from how others respond.

A truth voiced may unsettle the equilibrium of a relationship. Friends may not know how to receive it; families may feel confronted; colleagues may grow uneasy.

This discomfort is real, but it is not a signal to retreat. Rather, it shows the transformative power of honesty-how it shakes patterns and invites new ways of relating. In these moments, pain is paired with possibility.

The Liberation of Truth

Yet even as pain arises, honesty also carries immense freedom. It frees us from the weight of performance, from the strain of pretending, from the exhaustion of endless agreement. A single honest word can dissolve layers of tension.

A simple truth admitted can quiet a restless mind. In honesty, energy once spent on concealment is released into authenticity. We feel lighter, not because life is suddenly easier, but because we are no longer split between the self we show and the self we live.

Freedom appears first as relief. To finally say, *This is who I am* is to breathe more deeply than before.

To confess, *I do not know,* or *I am afraid,* or *I desire something else,* is to stand in alignment with what is real.

These truths may not solve everything, but they return us to wholeness. They remind us that authenticity is not perfection, but congruence-the outer life reflecting the inner.

Honesty also unlocks intimacy. When we dare to be seen as we truly are, we invite others to do the same.

Trust deepens not through endless harmony but through courageous honesty. Friendships become sturdier when truth can be spoken without fear. Partnerships grow more resilient when vulnerability replaces pretense.

Even in workplaces and communities, honesty creates cultures of trust, where people feel free to contribute authentically rather than hide behind roles. The freedom of honesty ripples outward, strengthening bonds rather than breaking them.

The paradox of honesty is that what begins as pain often ends as liberation.

The sting of exposure gives way to the relief of alignment. The discomfort of dismantling illusions gives way to the clarity of living in truth.

The unease of disrupting relationships gives way to the depth of genuine connection. Pain and freedom are not separate stages; they are interwoven threads. Each honest admission may ache at first, but it also carves a path toward a lighter, truer life.

It is important to remember that honesty is not an all-or-nothing act.

It unfolds in layers, like a spiral. We reveal what we are ready to reveal, to ourselves and to others. Each step of honesty prepares the way for the next, each truth spoken strengthens our capacity for deeper truth. The process is gradual, compassionate, and deeply human.

In the end, the pain and freedom of honesty remind us of a larger truth: that we were not born to live hidden.

Life calls us toward transparency, toward alignment, toward the courage of being known.

And though the path of honesty asks much of us, it offers even more in return-the liberation of living as we are, without disguise, without division, fully alive in the light of truth.

Accepting Imperfection as Strength

The mirror of truth does not only reveal hidden longings or unspoken fears.

It also reflects the marks and blemishes of being human-the mistakes made, the flaws carried, the uneven edges that never quite fit into the polished image we try to project.

At first, these imperfections can feel like proof of inadequacy. Yet with time and awareness, they reveal themselves as sources of strength, threads that make the fabric of our lives both resilient and real.

Perfection has long been held as a silent standard. From early years, we are rewarded for flawless performance, tidy answers, smooth presentations. Imperfection is often met with correction, sometimes with shame, rarely with celebration. And so, we learn to hide it.

We erase errors quickly, cover missteps with smiles, smooth out the stories we tell others so they appear seamless. The mirror, however, has no interest in illusions. It shows the full picture-cracks, scars, and all.

To accept these imperfections is not resignation; it is courage. It means acknowledging that the very cracks we wish to hide are the same places where light enters.

Every mistake carries a lesson, every flaw carries humanity, every scar carries evidence of survival. Without them, our stories would be sterile, lacking depth. With them, our lives carry texture, authenticity, and strength.

Imperfection as Connection

Consider the resilience born from failure. A person who has never stumbled may appear confident, but their foundation is untested.

The one who has fallen and risen carries a steadiness that cannot be faked. Their imperfection becomes their strength, for it proves their ability to endure, to adapt, to begin again.

The mirror that reflects these moments does not condemn; it honors the journey.

Imperfection also deepens connection. We may believe that others admire us most when we seem flawless, yet true intimacy often arises when we reveal our vulnerabilities.

A friend admits their struggle, and suddenly we feel safe to share ours. A leader confesses uncertainty, and trust in them grows stronger. A parent apologizes for a mistake, and a child learns that love is not diminished by error. In each case, imperfection becomes the bridge between souls. The mirror that reveals our flaws also reflects our shared humanity.

The pursuit of perfection, by contrast, often isolates. When we hide every crack, we create a polished surface that others cannot touch.

It may earn admiration, but it rarely invites closeness. Imperfection softens us. It makes us approachable, relatable, real. The courage to accept our flaws is also the courage to invite others nearer, to let relationships rest on authenticity rather than performance.

From Weakness to Strength

Psychologically, embracing imperfection releases immense pressure. Perfectionism fuels anxiety, a constant vigilance that drains energy. To accept imperfection is to step out of that cycle, to breathe more freely.

It does not mean carelessness or neglect; it means recognizing that growth is more valuable than flawlessness, that presence is richer than perfection.

The relief that follows is not laziness-it is liberation. It is the freedom to try, to learn, to live without the paralyzing fear of error.

Imperfection also shapes creativity. Art, music, and innovation rarely emerge from rigid perfection.

They spring from exploration, from trial and error, from the willingness to risk imperfection in pursuit of expression.

A wrong note can spark a new melody. A failed attempt can inspire a breakthrough. A flawed story can reveal deeper truths. The mirror of truth, when embraced fully, reminds us that imperfection is not an obstacle to creativity-it is its birthplace.

Accepting imperfection as strength requires a shift in perspective. Instead of seeing flaws as marks against us, we begin to see them as marks of life lived fully. Instead of hiding scars, we see them as records of healing. Instead of condemning mistakes, we treat them as teachers.

This shift does not erase the challenges of imperfection-it transforms them. What once felt like evidence of weakness becomes a testament to courage.

The empowering message within this acceptance is simple: to be imperfect is to be human, and to be human is to be strong.

Our strength does not lie in appearing flawless but in carrying our imperfections with dignity, learning from them, and allowing them to connect us to others.

The mirror of truth reflects this strength back to us, reminding us that authenticity shines brighter than polish, and resilience is more enduring than perfection.

When we finally meet our imperfections with compassion, we discover a paradox: what once felt heavy becomes light, what once felt shameful becomes liberating.

In accepting imperfection, we stop fighting against ourselves. We integrate every part of our being-the smooth and the rough, the triumphs and the stumbles-into a whole that is more powerful than any idealized image.

And in that wholeness, we find a deeper kind of perfection: not the absence of flaws, but the presence of truth.

CHAPTER 5

FIRES THAT CLEANSE

Life rarely moves in straight, gentle lines. There are seasons when the sky within us darkens, when the winds of circumstance rise and sweep away the structures we thought were unshakable.

These storms arrive in many forms: a sudden loss, a relationship unraveling, a career collapsing, a health challenge that alters everything. To the outside world, they look like disruptions.

To the inner world, they feel like breaking points. And yet, beneath their fury, storms carry an invitation-an opening to transformation.

Storms are not punishments. They are messengers. They arrive not to diminish us, but to reveal where we have been living too small, too tightly, too far from ourselves. Mental health, in particular, often shifts at these moments.

The breakdown of familiar patterns makes space for deeper awareness. The mind, overwhelmed by strain, calls us to pause, to listen, to rebuild on foundations that are truer and more sustainable. The storm, in all its chaos, becomes a teacher.

Storms also have a way of gathering what we have ignored. Unspoken sadness, postponed decisions, forgotten dreams-all of these rise to the surface when the winds blow hard enough.

In this way, the storm does not simply destroy; it rearranges. It takes what was hidden and places it in the open, forcing us to look, to feel, and to respond. What once could be avoided is now undeniable, and in that undeniable space lies the chance to change.

The Breaking and the Opening

In the midst of the storm, the experience feels anything but empowering.

Anxiety heightens, grief spreads through the body, anger simmers without clear release. The routines that once held us steady collapse like fragile scaffolding.

Yet within the breaking lies the opening. When the outer structures fall, the inner self is revealed. What we avoided rises into view, asking for acknowledgment.

What we suppressed speaks in voices we can no longer ignore.

A person who has lived behind constant achievement may suddenly face burnout so profound that rest becomes unavoidable.

In that forced stillness, they begin to ask: *What am I really chasing?* Someone who has silenced grief for years may find themselves undone by a single memory.

In that release, they discover the humanity of their own heart. A storm strips away illusions, and in doing so, it offers clarity.

Storms also strip away comparison. In difficult seasons, the façade of keeping up with others often crumbles. We stop measuring ourselves against polished images and begin to confront our own truth.

This too is cleansing-the realization that life is not about matching someone else's pace, but about moving at the rhythm of our own becoming.

The turning point arrives when we stop fighting the storm as an enemy and begin to see it as a threshold. Yes, it shakes us, but it also clears away what no longer serves. Yes, it hurts, but it also softens what had grown rigid. The storm cleanses not by destroying, but by preparing the ground for something new. What once felt like devastation reveals itself, over time, as purification.

Rising from the Ashes

This is why so many speak of their hardest seasons as the times that transformed them most deeply. The fire of loss, the weight of depression, the upheaval of change-all of these can become crucibles. They burn away what is false and reveal what is indestructible. They strip us to essentials, so that when we rise again, we do so not from performance but from authenticity.

The resilience that follows a storm is different from the strength we show in calm days. It is quieter, steadier, forged in fire. It carries humility, because we know how fragile life can be. It carries depth, because we have faced ourselves in the rawest of states. And it carries compassion, because storms remind us that everyone we meet is carrying battles we cannot see.

From the ashes of storms, new clarity arises. Many discover values they had overlooked-family, health, creativity, presence. Others find themselves drawn to simplify life, letting go of clutter, of noise, of endless striving. What seemed like loss becomes the soil for authenticity, for meaning, for peace.

In the language of healing, storms are not the end of the story-they are turning points. They awaken the dormant parts of us, expand our capacity for empathy, and teach us the value of presence. They remind us that growth is not about avoiding difficulty, but about moving through it with awareness. Each storm becomes a spiral step inward, leading us closer to our authentic core.

Life storms, though fierce, are not only chapters of pain. They are passages of becoming. They strip us down, they clear our vision, and they point us back to the truths we had forgotten. And when the winds finally still, we realize that we have been reshaped-not into someone else, but into more of who we truly are. In that realization, the storm fulfills its purpose: not to destroy, but to cleanse, to awaken, and to guide us home to ourselves.

The Hidden Power of Difficult Emotions

When storms sweep through the landscape of our lives, they often leave behind strong emotions-grief that aches, anger that burns, breakdowns that feel like collapse. These emotions can seem overwhelming, yet they carry a hidden power. They are not intruders meant to destroy us; they are purifiers, clearing the air of what has long been suppressed. Grief, anger, and breakdowns remind us that what is unacknowledged will always find a way to rise, and in rising, they cleanse.

Grief is the echo of love. It shows us what mattered, what touched us deeply enough to leave an absence we feel in our bones. While the world may tell us to move quickly past it, grief insists on presence. It asks us to pause, to honor the depth of our bond, to acknowledge that our hearts are capable of attachment so profound that their loss changes us. In this acknowledgment, grief purifies the heart. It clears the residue of denial and brings us closer to what we value most.

Anger as a Call to Integrity

Anger, too, often wears a misunderstood face. We are taught to suppress it, to keep it polite, to smile when flames burn inside. Yet anger, when listened to, points us toward boundaries crossed, injustices endured, truths ignored. It rises as a guardian of our integrity, demanding that we notice where something has gone wrong. Like fire, it can scorch when left uncontrolled, but when directed with awareness, it becomes a purifying force. It clears the debris of passivity, reawakens courage, and pushes us toward change.

A person who feels anger in the face of unfairness is not broken; they are alive to justice. Someone who feels fury when silenced is not weak; they are attuned to their own voice longing to be heard. Anger clarifies what matters. It burns away the fog of compliance and reveals the clear lines of self-respect. In this way, anger is less about destruction and more about reclamation-the reclaiming of one's truth, one's dignity, one's voice.

Breakdowns as Thresholds

Breakdowns are perhaps the most feared of all. They arrive when the weight of carrying too much for too long finally tips us into collapse. The body weakens, the mind refuses to cooperate, tears come uninvited. At first, this feels like failure. Yet breakdowns are not endings; they are thresholds. They force us to stop moving in directions that are unsustainable. They dismantle the structures we built on pretense and ask us to rebuild on authenticity.

A breakdown clears away the illusions of strength defined only as endurance. It reminds us that true strength includes softness, rest, and the courage to be vulnerable. In this sense, breakdowns purify by emptying us of what no longer serves. They strip away the excess and return us to the essentials: breath, presence, and the quiet recognition that we are still here, still capable of beginning again.

The Cleansing Flame

Together, grief, anger, and breakdowns act as elements of an inner fire. Each burns in its own way, yet each clears space for renewal. Grief softens the heart, teaching compassion. Anger sharpens the spirit, teaching integrity. Breakdowns humble the body and mind, teaching surrender. They do not leave us untouched, but they leave us truer. They burn away the lies we tell ourselves, the weight we should not have carried, the silence we should not have kept.

This purification is not about pain for its own sake. It is about the transformation that follows. Just as forests regenerate after fire, our lives often find new growth after these inner blazes. We emerge with greater clarity about what matters, with resilience shaped by surviving the flames, with wisdom that could not have been learned in calm waters.

When we allow grief, anger, and breakdowns to do their work-not suppressing them, not fearing them, but listening-we discover their gift. They remind us that being human is not about perfection or endless composure. It is about allowing the full range of our emotions to move through us, trusting that each has its purpose. In their own fierce and beautiful way, these difficult emotions cleanse the path ahead, leaving us lighter, clearer, and more ready to live with authenticity.

The Classroom of Loss

Loss is one of life's most uninvited teachers. It enters quietly at times-a friendship fading, an opportunity slipping away-or it storms in with sudden force: the passing of a loved one, the collapse of a cherished dream, the ending of a chapter we thought would last forever. Though painful, loss also reveals truths we would not have seen otherwise. It teaches us about impermanence, about the fragile and precious nature of each moment, about the courage it takes to love deeply knowing that nothing is guaranteed.

Loss humbles us. It strips away illusions of control and reminds us that much of life unfolds beyond our design. Yet in this stripping, it also awakens gratitude. We learn to hold what remains with more tenderness. A conversation is no longer taken for granted. A shared meal becomes a quiet celebration. The smallest details-a laugh, a gesture, a sunrise-swell with new meaning. Loss teaches us that beauty often lives in the ordinary, and that love is not diminished by endings but honored by remembrance.

Conflict as a Mirror

Conflict, too, is a teacher, though it often arrives dressed in discomfort. Arguments with loved ones, disagreements in workplaces, tensions within communities-these clashes can feel like ruptures. Yet conflict, when engaged with awareness, holds up a mirror. It shows us where values differ, where needs are unmet, where truths have gone unspoken.

Conflict reveals the edges of relationship. It uncovers the unspoken boundaries we never knew we had. When we resist conflict, we may feel fractured; when we lean into it with openness, we discover opportunities for clarity and growth. A disagreement with a partner may reveal hidden fears. A workplace clash may highlight new solutions waiting to be seen. Even global conflicts remind us of the importance of dialogue, empathy, and the courage to stand for justice. Though difficult, conflict sharpens us. It pushes us to articulate who we are, what we need, and how we can meet others with respect.

Lessons Carved in Fire

Both loss and conflict bring us face to face with vulnerability. They dismantle the illusion that life can be controlled into neat and unshaken harmony. Instead, they remind us that growth often emerges through friction. Like metal shaped in flame, our character takes form in the heat of difficulty. These fires refine us, burning away complacency and awakening strength we did not know we carried.

One lesson that emerges is resilience-the recognition that even when something precious is taken or relationships strain, we can endure. Another is empathy. Loss softens us toward others who grieve. Conflict broadens our perspective, teaching us to listen to voices beyond our own. These lessons cannot be read in books alone; they are written into us through experience.

Loss also teaches us the depth of love. To grieve is to know that we have loved, and to love despite the possibility of loss is one of the bravest acts we can choose. Conflict teaches us the depth of truth. To face disagreement without collapsing into silence is to honor both ourselves and others. In both cases, the discomfort we feel points toward growth. The lessons are not in avoiding pain or disagreement, but in meeting them with courage and openness.

Carrying the Wisdom Forward

The wisdom gathered through loss and conflict does not end with us. It ripples outward. A parent who has faced loss may guide their children to appreciate fleeting moments more deeply. A leader shaped by conflict may foster spaces of dialogue and inclusion. A friend who has known grief may sit with another in silence, offering presence rather than platitudes. The wisdom is lived, not spoken alone.

These lessons remind us of the interconnectedness of all lives. What we endure becomes part of the collective story. Our resilience offers courage to others. Our compassion becomes a balm. Our willingness to face discomfort models strength that is not about perfection, but about authenticity.

Loss and conflict are not the teachers we seek, but they are often the ones that shape us most profoundly. They remind us of what matters, they strip away what does not, and they give us tools to live with deeper presence and honesty. In their wake, we are not left broken but reshaped-carrying lessons that expand our humanity and prepare us for the chapters yet to come.

The Forge of Hardship

Resilience is not born in the calm but in the storm. It is shaped not when life flows smoothly, but when we stand in the heat of challenge. Hardship, much like fire, has a dual nature: it can burn, and it can refine. In the midst of difficulties, our first instinct may be to shield ourselves, to escape the blaze. Yet if we look closer, fire also reveals itself as a forge-a place where hidden strength is awakened, where the raw material of our being is transformed into something stronger, more luminous, and more enduring.

The fire of hardship strips away what is unnecessary. When we are pressed by difficulty, we discover what truly matters. The distractions that once consumed us lose their weight. The opinions of others quiet against the urgency of survival. The surface layers peel back, leaving us face to face with our essence. It is here, in the clarity born of fire, that resilience begins to form.

Endurance and Renewal

Resilience does not mean the absence of struggle. It is the art of enduring and renewing, of bending without breaking, of allowing ourselves to be reshaped without losing our core. In fire, metal softens before it strengthens again. In the same way, we too are softened-through tears, through pauses, through moments of vulnerability-before we rise with new solidity.

Resilience is built when we permit ourselves to experience both fragility and recovery. We cry, and then we breathe again. We fall, and then we stand. Each cycle teaches the body and spirit that collapse is not the end, but a stage in becoming. In this rhythm of falling and rising, resilience grows quietly, steadily, until it becomes a companion we can trust in future storms.

The Gift of Perspective

The fires of difficulty also offer perspective. When life has tested us deeply, we see the world differently. Small irritations lose their power. Gratitude sharpens. We no longer measure life solely by ease but by authenticity. The person who has walked through fire knows the value of a gentle word, the blessing of ordinary days, the strength of community. This perspective becomes a shield-not of denial, but of clarity-that steadies us when future challenges arise.

Perspective also reminds us that resilience is not about individual toughness alone. It is about interconnection. In the fire, we often lean on others-friends who listen, communities that support, strangers who show kindness. These moments reveal that resilience grows not in isolation but in relationship. The bonds formed in hardship often become lifelong anchors, reminding us that strength is both within and between us.

From Survival to Growth

What makes resilience remarkable is not just survival, but the capacity to grow through adversity. Fire transforms raw metal into something more refined; in the same way, hardship refines our inner life. We emerge not only intact, but expanded. Our compassion deepens because we understand pain. Our confidence grows because we have faced difficulty and endured. Our creativity awakens because challenges force us to imagine new possibilities.

Resilience built in fire often carries a paradoxical softness. Those who have endured are not hardened into stone; they are softened into empathy. They know the weight of struggle, and so they do not dismiss the struggles of others. They know the fragility of life, and so they treasure its beauty more keenly. This is the quiet strength of resilience-it does not roar, it hums with humility.

Living the Lesson

Resilience is not a distant ideal; it is lived in the everyday. It shows itself in the person who chooses to begin again after loss. It shines in the one who carries scars with dignity. It breathes in communities that rebuild after devastation, in families that find laughter even after sorrow, in individuals who wake each morning with the will to try again. These are not grand gestures but steady acts of courage-the daily fires in which resilience is continually forged.

In this way, resilience becomes less about bouncing back to what was and more about stepping forward into what can be. The fire does not return us unchanged; it leaves its mark, and that mark becomes part of our strength. To live resiliently is to embrace that mark with grace, to let the lessons of fire shape us into beings who are not only survivors, but creators of meaning, carriers of light, and proof that from every blaze, new life can emerge.

The Ground After the Fire

Every storm, every fire, eventually passes. What once roared with heat and chaos quiets, leaving behind a landscape changed. At first, the view may seem stark-old structures gone, familiar patterns dismantled, the ground scattered with ashes. Yet if we pause and look more closely, we begin to see what the fire could not take. Certain truths remain, solid beneath the surface. These truths are the foundation upon which we rebuild.

The experience of fire teaches us discernment. We learn to see what is essential and what was only decoration. Often, the things we thought defined us-the roles, the achievements, the polished surfaces-fall away in the blaze. What endures are the deeper values: love, integrity, connection, faith, creativity, compassion. These remain, shining more clearly now because the clutter has been cleared. To rebuild on what remains true is to anchor life in these essentials.

Discovering the Unshakable

In the quiet that follows upheaval, we discover strength we did not realize was ours. Perhaps it is the loyalty of relationships that endured the storm. Perhaps it is the inner courage that carried us through sleepless nights. Perhaps it is the creativity that still sparks even in dark seasons. These are not new-they were always within us-but it often takes fire to uncover them. Rebuilding begins with honoring these unshakable truths.

This discovery is not about starting from nothing, but about starting from authenticity. Imagine a forest after wildfire. Though the ground appears bare, the soil is enriched, ready to support new growth. In the same way, when life strips us of what was temporary, the soil of our being is enriched with wisdom, clarity, and resilience. We rebuild not with fear but with gratitude for the truths that survived.

Building with Simplicity and Depth

When we begin to rebuild, our choices often change. We no longer feel compelled to stack our lives with endless pursuits or fill every corner with noise. Instead, we seek simplicity and depth. We say yes to what feels aligned and let go of what feels hollow. We invest time in relationships that nourish rather than drain, in work that brings meaning rather than just recognition, in practices that sustain rather than deplete.

This rebuilding is an act of alignment. It is the steady process of letting outer life reflect inner truth. A person who has learned the value of presence may begin to slow their pace, savoring moments that once rushed past. Someone who has realized the strength of vulnerability may build relationships on openness rather than performance. Communities that have endured hardship may rebuild not only infrastructure but also trust, weaving bonds of cooperation and empathy stronger than before.

The Beauty of Beginning Again

Rebuilding after fire is not about restoring what was; it is about creating what can be. There is beauty in this beginning again. It carries the freshness of possibility, the clarity of intention, the humility of knowing how fragile life can be. Each choice feels more deliberate, each step more meaningful. We no longer take resilience for granted; we embody it in the very act of building.

The process is not rushed. Just as nature takes time to regenerate, so do we. New shoots push slowly through the soil, just as new habits and perspectives take time to root. But each small act-choosing honesty, practicing gratitude, nurturing relationships-becomes part of the rebuilding. Over time, these small acts create a structure stronger than the one that stood before, because it is built on truth rather than illusion.

Living From the Core

Ultimately, to rebuild on what remains true is to live from the core. It is to let go of borrowed scripts and stand in our own story. It is to honor the lessons the fire has given us, not by clinging to the past but by carrying its wisdom forward. It is to live with clarity about what matters, courage to protect it, and compassion to share it.

In this way, rebuilding is not only personal but collective. When individuals rebuild on truth, families grow more authentic, workplaces more humane, communities more resilient. The ripple of one person's clarity expands outward, shaping cultures where honesty and compassion are valued. The personal act of rebuilding becomes a communal act of renewal.

What remains after fire is not less-it is more. It is distilled, clarified, strengthened. And when we rebuild on this ground, our lives are not only restored but transformed. They become testimonies of resilience, reminders that even after the fiercest flames, there is always a foundation waiting, strong and steady, upon which new life can grow.

CHAPTER 6

THE SILENCE THAT SPEAKS

Human beings are born with the full spectrum of emotions, yet many of us grow up without learning their language. We feel storms move through us-anger, sadness, longing, joy-but when asked to name them, words stumble. Instead, we say, *I'm fine,* or *It's nothing,* even when the heart is full. This gap between what we feel and what we can express is called emotional illiteracy. It is not a lack of feeling but a lack of vocabulary, a silence that hides the depth of our inner life.

From childhood, we may have been told to be strong, to stop crying, to hide anger, to keep peace. Slowly, words for our emotions shrink from our daily speech. Happiness and sadness remain, perhaps anger and love, but the subtler shades vanish. We know irritation but not disappointment, we know excitement but not anticipation, we know sorrow but not yearning. Without names, these feelings remain shadows-present but unnamed, heavy yet invisible.

The Cost of Silence

The inability to name emotions does not make them disappear. Instead, they move underground, shaping our choices without our awareness. A person unable to recognize envy may disguise it as irritation. Someone who cannot name grief may carry it as fatigue. Another who does not know how to describe anxiety may call it restlessness or simply "stress." The silence does not protect us; it blinds us.

Emotional illiteracy also distances us from one another. How can we share our world if we cannot describe it? Relationships weaken when conversations stop at the surface. A partner who cannot express hurt may withdraw instead. A child who cannot describe fear may act out. A friend unable to voice loneliness may appear indifferent. Words are bridges, and without them, the distance between hearts widens.

Rediscovering the Vocabulary of the Heart

Learning to name feelings is not about acquiring a dictionary-it is about cultivating awareness. It begins with pausing to listen. What stirs in me right now? Is this irritation, or is it disappointment? Is this nervousness, or is it anticipation? Is this calm, or is it numbness? Asking these questions slows the rush of automatic living and allows us to touch the subtleties of our experience.

Journaling can be a gentle practice for rediscovery. When we write, we are invited to search for precise words. Over time, the vocabulary grows, and with it, the clarity of self-understanding. Conversations deepen when we move beyond broad terms. Saying "I feel overlooked" lands differently than saying "I'm upset." Saying "I feel hopeful" carries more warmth than saying "I'm fine." Each word becomes a lantern, illuminating what was once dark.

The Power of Naming

When we name an emotion, something shifts inside us. The vague fog becomes a shape we can see and engage with. Neuroscientists call this *affect labeling*: the act of naming feelings reduces their intensity and increases our ability to regulate them. Spiritually and psychologically, naming is acknowledgment-it tells the inner self, *I see you, I hear you, you are real.*

Imagine a child learning to identify colors. At first, everything is simply "blue" or "red." Then they learn "turquoise," "scarlet," "indigo." The world becomes richer, more nuanced. The same happens with emotions. What we once called sadness may reveal itself as nostalgia, loneliness, or grief. What we called happiness may reveal itself as contentment, excitement, or awe. The inner world expands with every word learned.

Toward Emotional Fluency

Emotional fluency is not perfection-it is presence. It is not about controlling every feeling but recognizing them with honesty. It allows us to communicate with depth, to connect with compassion, to live with authenticity. A person fluent in emotions is not someone who never struggles, but someone who knows how to say, *This is what I feel, this is where I am.*

The silence of emotional illiteracy does not have to be permanent. It can be softened through curiosity, expanded through practice, transformed into fluency. As we learn to name our feelings, we reclaim our voices. We become more whole, more connected, more alive. And in that simple act of naming, silence begins to speak-clearly, powerfully, beautifully.

The Weight Without Words

There is a kind of silence that settles not in the room but in the soul. It is heavy, like air before a storm, thick with what cannot be said. This is the silence of depression-the unspoken heaviness that lingers when emotions remain unnamed, when pain is carried inward, hidden from view. To the outside world, life may appear intact: tasks completed, conversations managed, routines followed. Yet beneath the surface, the weight persists, pressing down on energy, dimming joy, dulling color.

Depression is often misunderstood because it wears many disguises. It may appear as fatigue that no rest relieves, as detachment in places where laughter once flowed, as stillness that feels less like peace and more like absence. The difficulty is not only in the heaviness itself, but in the silence surrounding it. For many, the words to describe it remain elusive. When asked how they feel, the response may be simply, *I don't know.* And in that not knowing, the heaviness deepens.

The Quiet Drift

This unspoken heaviness is rarely sudden. It builds gradually, like shadows lengthening at dusk. At first, one might notice only a lack of spark-books unread, music unplayed, conversations shorter. Slowly, the quiet spreads. Tasks that once felt simple begin to require effort. Even joy, when it arrives, feels muted, as though experienced through a veil. This quiet drift often goes unnoticed by others, and sometimes even by the one experiencing it, until the silence grows too loud to ignore.

The tragedy of this silence is that it convinces us we are alone in it. Because the weight has no easy words, we assume it cannot be shared. Yet across the world, countless others carry the same hidden burden, waiting for language, waiting for recognition. Depression thrives in the unspoken, but it begins to soften when brought into voice.

The Language of Heaviness

Finding words for depression is less about medical terms and more about metaphors of the heart. Some describe it as walking through fog, others as carrying stones in their chest, still others as moving underwater. These images may not be precise, but they capture the texture of the experience. They give shape to the shapeless and open doors to understanding.

When someone says, *I feel heavy,* they are not describing weakness. They are describing the weight of silence that has built within them. When they say, *Everything feels gray,* they are not dramatic-they are naming the dulling of joy. Language does not remove the heaviness, but it creates space around it, making it less suffocating. In speaking, the silence begins to shift.

The Hidden Courage

Living with unspoken heaviness requires courage, even when it does not feel like it. Each day carried forward is an act of resilience. Each moment of reaching for connection, even when words falter, is an act of bravery. Depression often tells a person they are weak, yet the very fact of enduring proves otherwise. Strength is not in pretending the heaviness is absent-it is in acknowledging it and still moving through life with as much presence as possible.

This perspective reframes the silence. Rather than a void, it can be seen as a space awaiting voice. Rather than emptiness, it can be seen as a pause before expression. The courage lies in turning toward the heaviness with curiosity: *What is this weight trying to tell me? What part of me has been silenced too long?* In these questions, the silence begins to speak.

Toward Gentle Openings

The path out of unspoken heaviness is not always quick, but it begins with small openings. Speaking even a fragment of truth-*I feel tired in ways I can't explain,* or *Something feels heavy inside me*-can create space for healing. Journaling, therapy, trusted friendships, or even quiet self-reflection can provide containers where the silence is welcomed rather than dismissed.

Gentleness is essential. Depression often convinces us that we should recover faster, speak more clearly, move more quickly. Yet healing grows best in softness. Allowing ourselves to rest, to feel, to name only what we can in the moment-these are not signs of failure but of wisdom. Just as a fire needs time to burn down before new growth can sprout, the heaviness needs patience before it lightens.

The Whisper of Hope

Even within silence, a whisper of hope remains. The heaviness is not the end of the story. It is a signal that something within us is asking for recognition, for care, for new ways of being. When we begin to listen, when we dare to find words, when we reach toward others, the silence slowly transforms. The heaviness, once suffocating, becomes a teacher-reminding us of our need for connection, compassion, and authenticity.

Depression as unspoken heaviness does not define us. It is a chapter, not the whole book. Within it lies the possibility of renewal. And though the silence may feel immovable, even the heaviest clouds eventually part, letting light through. The work is not to force the sun to shine, but to stay open until it does-to keep listening, keep naming, and keep trusting that even in silence, life continues to move toward healing.

The Mask of Composure

Loneliness is one of the most paradoxical human experiences. It thrives not only in isolation but also in crowded rooms, in workplaces full of chatter, in families gathered around dinner tables. Many who carry loneliness wear it beneath a mask of composure. Their faces remain calm, their voices steady, their lives seemingly intact. Yet behind the quiet, an ache lingers-the longing to be seen, known, and understood. These quiet faces rarely reveal the fullness of their solitude, making loneliness one of the most hidden forms of silence.

Often, society rewards composure. We admire those who appear steady, who do not burden others with their struggles, who seem endlessly self-sufficient. But beneath this steadiness, many carry the quiet weight of feeling invisible. Loneliness is not simply the absence of company; it is the absence of recognition. It is the experience of sitting beside others yet feeling that no one truly notices the depths within you.

The Disguise of Daily Life

Loneliness hides itself in routines. A colleague may arrive at work, exchange pleasantries, complete tasks, and go home, all while feeling untouched by real connection. A parent may care for children tirelessly, surrounded by noise, yet feel unseen in their own needs. A student may laugh with peers but silently wonder if anyone truly knows their heart. From the outside, nothing appears amiss. The face is quiet, the demeanor collected. Inside, the silence grows louder.

This hidden loneliness is often unspoken because naming it feels risky. To say *I feel lonely* can sound like weakness, as though it means one is unloved or unwanted. Yet loneliness is not a verdict on worth-it is a signal of unmet need, the need for authentic presence. When we misunderstand it, we bury it deeper, layering smiles over the ache. And so the quiet faces remain, admired for their calm, while carrying a solitude that words have not yet freed.

The Subtle Signals

Though hidden, loneliness leaves traces. It appears in the sigh released when the day finally ends. It lives in the longing glance toward a group in laughter, the hesitation before reaching out to call a friend. It lingers in the scroll through social media, not out of interest but out of yearning to feel connected. These signals may be small, but together they paint a portrait of longing.

Recognizing these signals-within ourselves and others-creates space for compassion. To notice that someone's quiet may be more than peace, that their solitude may be more than preference, is to begin to bridge the gap. Loneliness does not demand dramatic gestures. Often, it asks simply for presence: for someone to listen without rushing, to see without judgment, to share without expectation.

Rediscovering Connection

The silence of loneliness begins to shift when we dare to reach beyond the mask. It may start with a single word-*I miss you, I wish we talked more, Sometimes I feel alone even when I'm with people.* These admissions, though vulnerable, carry immense power. They invite others into the hidden room of our hearts. They remind us that loneliness is not a personal flaw but a universal experience, one that eases when shared.

Connection does not require constant company; it requires authenticity. A brief but genuine conversation can heal more than hours of surface chatter. A moment of shared laughter, a pause to truly listen, a willingness to be seen as we are-these are the threads that mend the fabric of belonging. For the quiet faces, what heals is not noise but recognition, not crowds but closeness.

The Quiet Gift

While loneliness is often painful, it also carries a quiet gift. It heightens our awareness of connection's value. Those who have known deep solitude often become the most attentive companions, the most compassionate listeners, the ones who notice what others overlook. In this way, loneliness refines us, teaching us not only the ache of absence but also the beauty of presence.

To acknowledge loneliness is to let the silence speak. It is to honor the truth behind the quiet faces and to offer them-ourselves included-the grace of recognition. When we do, loneliness transforms from a hidden ache into a doorway: a doorway back to connection, to empathy, and to the profound relief of being seen.

The Words We Lost

There is a language we are all meant to inherit-a vocabulary of the heart. It should have been handed down alongside alphabets and numbers, teaching us how to name the tremors within. Yet for many, this vocabulary was stolen, not by malice but by silence. We were told to be strong instead of tender, to be agreeable instead of honest, to be calm instead of expressive. In this way, the dictionary of emotions was thinned, leaving us fluent in outer achievement but tongue-tied in inner truth.

Without words, feelings remain shadows. A child who is sad but only knows the word *angry* grows up expressing sorrow through irritation. A teenager who feels shame but cannot name it may hide behind arrogance. An adult who longs for connection but lacks the vocabulary may settle for surface conversation. The theft of words is the theft of clarity. Without them, emotions swirl unnamed, shaping choices without our awareness.

The Power of Naming

To reclaim our vocabulary is to reclaim ourselves. Naming emotions is not indulgence-it is precision. When we say, *I feel anxious,* we touch one layer of truth. When we say,

I feel vulnerable because I fear being judged, we add depth, texture, clarity. Each word refines the picture, turning a blur into a portrait. Neuroscience tells us that labeling feelings reduces their intensity, but lived experience shows us something deeper: naming creates connection. It bridges the inner world and the outer, making us known to ourselves and to others.

Think of emotions as colors. Without vocabulary, we live in black and white-happy or sad, angry or calm. With vocabulary, the spectrum expands: melancholy, nostalgia, anticipation, serenity, awe. Suddenly life becomes richer, each shade distinct, each experience honored. Emotional vocabulary is not decoration; it is illumination. It helps us see ourselves more clearly and live more authentically.

Practices of Reclaiming

Unlocking the stolen vocabulary begins with curiosity. When a wave of feeling rises, pause. Instead of pushing it away, ask: *What is this? What is its texture? What word feels close?* At first, the answers may be broad-*tired, sad, restless.* But over time, more nuanced words emerge-*disheartened, yearning, apprehensive, relieved.* Every new word adds a key to the lexicon, opening another door into self-understanding.

Journaling can be a gentle companion in this journey. On paper, we are free to experiment with words, to search for the right ones, to notice patterns. Conversations, too, become classrooms. When we listen to others describe their feelings, we collect new language for our own. Poetry, stories, and art can also restore stolen words, giving us metaphors when literal language feels too small.

The Gift of Shared Language

The beauty of expanding emotional vocabulary is not only personal-it is relational. When we articulate our emotions clearly, others can meet us more fully. Saying *I feel distant* invites a different response than saying *I'm fine.* Saying *I feel hopeful* creates more connection than silence. Shared language deepens trust. It assures others that they are not guessing at our truth; we are offering it freely.

For families, this can transform generations. Parents who model emotional vocabulary teach children that feelings are not threats but guides. Partners who share nuanced emotions build intimacy rooted in honesty. Communities that embrace the language of feelings foster compassion rather than judgment. Each word becomes a thread, weaving people closer together.

The Liberation of Voice

Reclaiming this vocabulary is an act of liberation. It frees us from silence, from the weight of carrying unnamed burdens. It restores to us the ability to say not only what we think, but what we feel. In doing so, we live more congruently-our outer lives reflecting our inner truth.

The stolen words can be unlocked. They were never lost forever, only waiting to be remembered. Each time we pause to notice, to name, to share, the silence breaks. The dictionary of the heart reopens, page by page, word by word. And as it does, we find ourselves not only more articulate, but more whole-able to stand in the fullness of our humanity, speaking clearly the language of the soul.

The Weight of the Unsaid

Every life holds words that were swallowed. Feelings left unspoken, truths set aside, experiences hidden in the corners of memory. These unsaid things linger, carrying a quiet weight. At first, silence feels safer: safer than conflict, safer than rejection, safer than being misunderstood. Yet over time, the unspeakable becomes heavy, pressing on the chest, echoing in the mind, shaping choices without our awareness. The silence that once protected us becomes a binding.

To speak what was once unspeakable is an act of release. It does not erase the past, but it frees the present. It allows the voice, long muted, to rise and find resonance again. It takes courage, because the unspeakable is often tangled with fear-fear of judgment, of change, of hurting others, of stepping outside the roles we were trained to play. And yet, when the words finally emerge, they do more than liberate us; they ripple outward, changing the spaces we inhabit.

The First Voice

Breaking silence rarely happens in grand declarations. It begins with a whisper: *I felt hurt. I need more support. I carry this memory.* The first voice often trembles, but trembling is not weakness-it is the vibration of walls loosening, of barriers beginning to fall. Each time we dare to name what has lived in shadow, we make space for honesty, and honesty heals.

Sometimes the first unspeakable words are spoken only to ourselves. Writing in a journal, standing before a mirror, or simply thinking, *This is my truth.* Acknowledgment precedes expression. Once we accept our own voice internally, it becomes easier to share it outwardly-with a friend, a partner, a community. The process is gradual, but each step widens the circle of freedom.

The Healing Power of Expression

When what was once unspeakable is spoken, something remarkable occurs: the weight shifts. Words that seemed unbearable when held inside become lighter when shared. Others may nod in recognition, may say *me too,* may offer comfort we never expected. The story that felt isolating reveals itself as universal. Expression does not always guarantee agreement or immediate resolution, but it always opens the door to connection.

This is the alchemy of voice. Pain turns into purpose when spoken. Secrets transform into bridges when revealed. Even anger, when expressed with clarity rather than aggression, becomes a force for justice rather than destruction. To speak is to reframe the narrative, to say: *This experience shapes me, but it does not define me in silence.*

Voices as Invitations

The unspeakable, once voiced, becomes an invitation for others. When someone admits loneliness, another feels permission to share theirs. When someone confesses fear, others find the courage to reveal their own. When someone tells the story of survival, those still struggling feel less alone. Our voice becomes not just a release for ourselves, but a lantern for others in the dark.

In families, this can heal generations. A parent who speaks honestly about their struggles models resilience for their children. In workplaces, leaders who acknowledge vulnerability create cultures of trust. In communities, collective voices break stigma and open paths for change.

The act of speaking what was once unspeakable reshapes not only the self but also the world around us.

The Beauty of Living in Truth

The freedom of speech is not only political-it is deeply personal. To give voice to the unspeakable is to live in alignment, where the inner and outer self finally meet. The voice says what the heart knows, and in that unity, peace grows. We no longer spend energy hiding, pretending, or suppressing. Instead, we live with congruence, with integrity, with the quiet confidence of authenticity.

Speaking does not mean shouting every thought or emotion. It means choosing moments of honesty, offering truths with compassion, trusting that silence is no longer our only option. It means living in a way that honors the full spectrum of our humanity-the parts that are strong and the parts that are tender, the parts that are certain and the parts that are uncertain.

The unspeakable loses its power when spoken. What once felt too heavy to carry becomes lighter in the air, transformed by sound, witnessed by others, integrated into the story of who we are. And in that act of speaking, silence itself changes-it becomes not the weight of what we hide, but the pause that gives meaning to the words we now dare to say.

INTERLUDE I: LETTER TO SELF-WHAT AM I AFRAID TO HEAR?

Take a pause here. Close the noise of the world for a moment. Let this page become a mirror, a quiet room where only you and your inner voice are present.

This is not a test, not a task-it is an invitation. An invitation to listen to the truths that often whisper but rarely get the chance to speak.

Imagine you are writing a letter, not to anyone else, but to yourself. Begin with gentleness.

Dear me... or *To the one still learning...*

Allow the words to flow as though you are both the writer and the recipient. What would you tell yourself if you trusted that no judgment could follow?

What would you admit if you knew that honesty would only bring relief?

Ask yourself:

What am I afraid to hear?

Is it a longing I have silenced? A boundary I wish to set? A dream I still carry quietly? A truth about how tired I feel, how much I need rest, how deeply I want joy? Write it down.

Let the ink carry what the lips hesitate to say.

This exercise is not about answers. It is about presence. When you name the things you are afraid to hear, you create space for them to soften.

You may discover that the truth is less frightening on the page than it was in silence. You may notice a sense of clarity rising, as though the fog begins to lift.

If words feel difficult, try starting with a single phrase:

I wish... I need... I miss... I hope...

Let the sentence finish itself, without correction. Trust what arrives. Each line is a doorway to the self you have been carrying quietly all along.

When you are ready, close the letter with kindness. Offer yourself the words you most long to hear from another:

I believe in you. You are allowed to rest. You are stronger than you realize.

These closing lines are not promises of perfection-they are reminders of worth, the gentle hands that hold you steady as you continue.

Keep this letter. Return to it when silence feels heavy. It will remind you that your voice is not lost, only waiting.

And each time you dare to write again, the unsaid truths will find their way into the light, one sentence at a time.

PART III

THE LISTENING

CHAPTER 7

CIRCLES OF PROTECTION

Imagine standing in the center of a circle drawn gently around you. This circle is not a wall of stone, nor a fence of iron. It is light-soft yet steady, permeable yet protective.

Within it, you can breathe more freely. Within it, you are reminded: this space belongs to you.

This is the essence of boundaries. They are not acts of rejection; they are acts of care. They are tools that preserve mental health by helping us honor both our energy and our relationships.

Boundaries exist in every healthy ecosystem. Rivers have banks to guide their flow, trees have bark to protect their core, even the human body has skin that allows contact while shielding what is tender.

Just as nature thrives within its boundaries, so do we. Without them, we feel depleted, scattered, overexposed.

With them, we gain clarity, steadiness, and the capacity to engage with the world in ways that are sustainable.

Why Boundaries Heal

The mind and heart need containers to hold their strength. Without boundaries, we may say yes when we mean no, give when our reserves are empty, or remain silent when our truth longs to be voiced.

Each of these small compromises may seem harmless at first, but over time they drain vitality. Mental health suffers not only from external stress but also from the absence of inner protection.

Boundaries act as guardians.

They tell us where we end and another begins. They remind us that care is not endless sacrifice, but balance.

To say *no* is not cruelty-it is an affirmation that our energy has value.

To step back is not abandonment-it is trust that relationships can hold space for difference. Boundaries make space for authenticity. They invite us to meet others with honesty instead of resentment, with presence instead of exhaustion.

The Practice of Drawing Circles

Creating boundaries begins with awareness. Notice the moments when your body tenses, when your energy feels drained, when irritation surfaces unexpectedly.

These are signals. They often mean that your inner circle has been crossed, that you have given beyond comfort or allowed entry where caution was needed. Listening to these signals is the first act of boundary-making.

Start with small, clear steps. Instead of overexplaining, practice saying,

I'm not available right now, or *I need some time for myself.*

Instead of carrying others' responsibilities, try,

I trust you to handle this.

Boundaries grow stronger through repetition, like muscles trained gently over time. Each time you draw the circle, you reinforce your ability to live within it.

This practice does not isolate you. Rather, it allows you to connect from a place of fullness.

When your circle is intact, you give with joy instead of resentment, listen with openness instead of fatigue, and love with presence instead of depletion. Boundaries do not shrink love; they make it sustainable.

Boundaries as Invitations

Perhaps the most surprising truth is that boundaries benefit not only ourselves but also those around us.

When we honor our own needs, we model respect for others to do the same. When we are clear about our limits, relationships grow stronger because they rest on honesty rather than assumption.

Boundaries are invitations to meet one another as whole beings, not as fragments offered in exhaustion.

Think of friendships built on mutual understanding of space and closeness, partners who can honor both intimacy and individuality, workplaces where limits are respected and creativity thrives.

In each case, boundaries do not divide-they create conditions for trust. They are the invisible agreements that allow connection to flourish.

Living Inside the Circle

Boundaries as mental health tools remind us that self-care is not selfish. It is the foundation upon which all genuine care rests.

To live inside your circle is to live with intention: giving when you have energy, pausing when you need rest, speaking when truth rises, listening when presence is enough.

This balance protects your mental health and enriches every bond you hold.

So, stand again in the circle of light around you.

Feel its steadiness. Let it remind you that your well-being matters, that your energy has worth, that your voice deserves space.

From this circle, you can meet the world with more clarity, more compassion, more resilience. Boundaries are not barriers-they are bridges, connecting us to others while keeping us anchored to ourselves.

Circles Across Civilizations

Throughout history, communities have instinctively created rituals and spaces that protect the human spirit.

From the sacred fire circles of indigenous traditions to the communal courtyards of villages, from meditation halls in monasteries to tea ceremonies in quiet rooms, cultures across the world have understood that well-being requires more than survival-it requires sanctuary.

These practices were not framed as "mental health strategies," yet that is exactly what they offered: circles of safety where people could pause, share, and restore.

In many traditions, the circle itself is a symbol of protection. It holds no sharp edges, no hierarchy, no division between beginning and end.

Within a circle, people face one another as equals. Stories are told, songs are sung, silence is shared.

The shape itself invites safety, reminding us that protection is not about building walls but about creating spaces of connection, balance, and belonging.

Sacred Rituals of Safety

Consider the way indigenous communities gather around fire. The flames provide warmth and light, but they also create an invisible shield-a place where fears can be spoken, wisdom shared, and silence honored.

In this space, the fire becomes more than element; it becomes witness. It absorbs the unspoken and gives back clarity. Such circles remind us that protection is not isolation, but communion.

In Japanese tea ceremonies, the ritual of preparing and serving tea is less about the beverage and more about the atmosphere.

The room is arranged with care, the movements are deliberate, the silence is intentional.

This ritual creates a space where participants leave behind the noise of daily life and enter a field of presence. Here, safety comes not from boundaries of distance, but from the shared agreement to honor simplicity, attentiveness, and respect.

In African villages, the concept of *ubuntu*-"I am because we are"-creates safe spaces through community gatherings. Decisions are made collectively, children are raised with the support of many, and grief or joy is held by all.

These practices remind us that safety is not always private; often, it is woven through collective care.

The village circle is both protection and empowerment, teaching that well-being is sustained when carried together.

Modern Echoes

Though modern life often scatters us, echoes of these practices remain.

Support groups, community meals, yoga studios, and storytelling circles are contemporary ways of recreating what cultures have always known: that human beings need intentional spaces where vulnerability is welcomed and respect is assured.

Even digital spaces, when held with integrity, can mirror these traditions-online communities where people share openly, listen deeply, and offer compassion without judgment.

Workplaces, too, are slowly learning from cultural practices of safe space.

Circles of dialogue, mindful check-ins, and restorative practices are becoming ways to counter burnout and isolation. These are not trends but returns-returns to the understanding that people thrive when they feel protected, seen, and supported.

Creating Your Own Sanctuary

Safe space is not bound to any single culture; it is a universal human need. Each of us can draw from these practices to create circles of protection in daily life.

It may be as simple as setting aside a corner of the home for reflection, gathering friends regularly for intentional conversation, or practicing rituals that bring calm and clarity.

The key is intention: naming a space as sacred, even for a moment, transforms it from ordinary to restorative.

Ask yourself:

Where do I feel safe enough to exhale fully? Who are the people with whom my spirit rests easily? What rituals bring me back to center?

These questions help us recognize the cultural practices that resonate most with us and adapt them into our own lives.

The Shared Human Thread

Across cultures, the details differ, but the essence remains: people thrive in circles of protection.

Whether through firelight, tea, prayer, or song, humans have always found ways to create sanctuaries for the heart and mind.

These practices remind us that safe space is not a luxury-it is a necessity, a vital tool for resilience and wholeness.

As we carry these cultural teachings forward, we discover that creating safe space is not only about personal well-being but also about collective healing.

Each circle we form-whether in our families, communities, or workplaces-adds to the larger circle of humanity. And in that widening embrace, we find both protection and belonging.

The Sacred Pause

There comes a moment when the heart whispers what the lips hesitate to say:

enough.

Enough giving beyond our strength. Enough stretching beyond what feels true. Enough carrying what was never ours to hold.

To speak this word is not rebellion-it is restoration. It is the sacred pause that rebalances life, the drawing of a circle around our energy so that it may replenish.

And yet, for many, the act of saying *enough* is shadowed by guilt, as though protecting oneself is somehow betrayal.

But what if saying *enough* is not selfish, but an act of love-for ourselves, for our relationships, for the work we offer to the world?

The Burden of Guilt

Why does guilt so often follow when we set limits? Perhaps because we are taught from childhood that worth is tied to endless giving.

The student praised for never refusing. The employee rewarded for staying late. The parent admired for carrying everything without pause. The message is clear: to stop is to fail, to rest is to fall short. Over time, we learn to fear that saying *enough* means disappointing others or losing belonging.

But guilt in this context is not truth; it is conditioning.

It is the echo of expectations passed down through families, cultures, and systems that value productivity over presence. When we recognize guilt for what it is-a learned reflex-we can begin to loosen its hold.

The circle of protection grows stronger when we understand that our value is not measured by how much we endure, but by how authentically we live.

Redefining Enough

To say *enough* without guilt is to reframe the word itself. *Enough* does not mean refusal; it means honoring balance. It is not the end of giving, but the beginning of sustainable giving. When we say,

I have done enough for today,

we protect our well-being so that tomorrow's offerings can be genuine. When we say,

I have listened enough for now,

we safeguard our capacity to listen again with presence. Enough is not a barrier; it is a rhythm, a cadence that keeps life in harmony.

Consider nature: rivers know their banks, tides know their cycles, trees shed their leaves when the season calls for rest.

None of these pauses signal weakness-they are the wisdom of enough. We, too, are part of this rhythm. To honor our limits is to align ourselves with the very flow of life.

Practicing the Word

The courage to say *enough* grows with practice. At first, the word may feel heavy on the tongue. We may hear guilt whispering:

You are letting someone down.

But each time we speak it with clarity, the word softens. Begin with small steps.

Enough screen time for today. Enough tasks added to my plate. Enough conversations when my energy feels thin.

These simple practices strengthen the muscle of self-honor.

Over time, saying *enough* becomes less about turning away and more about turning inward. It becomes an act of listening deeply to the body, the mind, the heart. It becomes a way of saying,

I trust myself to know when my spirit needs pause.

And in that trust, guilt begins to dissolve.

The Ripple of Respect

What often surprises us is how others respond when we begin to say *enough*. Instead of rejection, many offer respect. Boundaries create clarity.

When we honor our limits, others know where we stand, and relationships grow sturdier. Colleagues learn to trust our yes because it is no longer automatic.

Friends feel safer sharing their own needs when they see us honoring ours. Children raised in homes where *enough* is spoken grow up knowing that love includes rest, that care includes self-care.

In this way, saying *enough* is not only for ourselves-it is a gift to everyone we touch. It models authenticity. It creates healthier bonds. It ensures that what we give is given freely, not from exhaustion but from fullness.

The Liberation of Enough

Imagine standing within your own circle of protection, the light around you glowing steady.

In this space, you know that your worth is not in constant doing. You know that rest is not laziness but wisdom.

You know that balance is not indulgence but strength. Here, the word *enough* feels liberating, not guilty. It is the reminder that life is not about carrying endlessly, but about carrying meaningfully.

When you next feel the weight of obligation pressing in, pause. Place a hand on your heart and ask:

Have I reached my enough for today?

Listen to the answer, even if it whispers. Trust it. Speaking that word will not close doors; it will open them-to health, to honesty, to harmony.

Enough is not the end. It is the beginning of living in rhythm with yourself.

The Dance Between Giving and Guarding

To live fully is to open ourselves-to love, to friendship, to community, to experience.

Yet to live wisely is to know that openness must be balanced with care for the self. Imagine openness as a window: when thrown wide, fresh air enters, light streams in, connection thrives. But without care, the same window can also let in storms, dust, and noise.

Balance is not about closing the window but about learning when to keep it wide, when to adjust the curtain, and when to rest in quiet.

Openness is a gift. It allows us to connect deeply, to share honestly, to feel the richness of belonging. But self-care is the ground on which that openness rests.

Without tending to ourselves, openness can become overexposure. With care, openness becomes sustainable, a practice that nourishes both us and those around us.

The Risks of Endless Openness

Many of us are taught to value openness as though it requires no limits: always available, always receptive, always saying yes.

While generosity of spirit is beautiful, without balance it drains us.

Constant openness can blur boundaries, leaving us unsure of where others end and we begin.

It may lead us to carry emotions that are not ours, to say yes when our bodies long for pause, to offer presence when our hearts are weary.

This does not mean openness is wrong-it means openness must be held with awareness. Just as the heart beats with rhythm-expansion and contraction-so must our emotional lives. Openness is expansion. Self-care is contraction.

Together, they create the rhythm of balance.

Practices of Gentle Balance

Balancing openness with self-care begins with listening inward. Notice how your body responds in different spaces.

Do you feel light and expansive in some conversations, yet heavy in others? Do you find joy in certain forms of giving, yet exhaustion in others?

These signals are guides. They tell you when openness enriches and when it overwhelms.

Practical rituals can help sustain this balance:

- **Set intentional limits**: Choose moments of openness rather than leaving the door always unguarded. A chosen yes is far more powerful than a reflexive one.
- **Create recovery spaces**: After deep conversations or social gatherings, give yourself time to rest. Solitude, journaling, or nature walks allow the heart to settle and replenish.
- **Practice mindful presence**: When with others, be fully open in that moment. When alone, be fully present with yourself. This alternation strengthens both connection and self-care.

The Circle as Companion

The metaphor of the circle returns here. Picture your openness radiating outward from the center of your circle.

Within the circle, you decide what to share, when to share, and with whom. The circle is not a barrier; it is a guide. It ensures that your openness flows with intention rather than compulsion. It reminds you that you can be both available and protected, both generous and discerning.

This circle also teaches that self-care is not withdrawal. It is the soil in which openness can flourish. When we rest, nourish ourselves, and listen inward, our capacity to connect expands.

Without self-care, openness can lead to depletion. With self-care, openness becomes radiant-clear, grounded, sustainable.

The Ripple of Balanced Living

When openness and self-care move in harmony, relationships deepen. Friends and partners feel the authenticity of your presence, knowing it comes not from obligation but from genuine choicc.

Work becomes more creative, because your energy is not scattered. Communities flourish, because each member contributes from a place of wholeness rather than exhaustion.

This balance ripples inward as well. You feel lighter, clearer, more aligned.

Instead of fearing that boundaries will make you distant, you discover that they make you more present. Instead of seeing self-care as indulgence, you understand it as the very foundation of your openness.

To balance openness with self-care is to honor both sides of being human: the longing to connect and the need to restore. It is to live in rhythm, like the tide that moves forward and retreats, like breath that inhales and exhales. When we honor this rhythm, we discover that openness does not diminish with boundaries-it strengthens, because it is rooted in care.

So let your window open wide when the sun is warm. Draw the curtain gently when storms gather.

Trust that balance is not withdrawal-it is wisdom.

And from that wisdom, your openness becomes not fragile but luminous, a gift you can offer again and again without losing yourself.

The Edge as Threshold

Every circle has an edge, a boundary where the familiar meets the unknown. For human beings, these edges are not just limits-they are thresholds. It is at the edges of our comfort, of our patience, of our energy, that resilience begins to take root. Inside the circle, we rest and replenish.

At its edge, we are stretched, tested, and shaped. Both are necessary: the sanctuary of safety and the threshold of growth.

Edges are often misunderstood. We think of them as barriers that confine us, or as places where danger waits. But edges are where life sharpens awareness.

They ask:

How will you hold your ground? How will you adapt when the familiar no longer guides you?

In meeting these questions, resilience is born-not in endless exposure, but in the dance between protection and challenge.

The Nature of Edges

Look at nature for guidance. The most diverse ecosystems thrive at edges: where forest meets meadow, where river meets ocean, where mountain touches plain.

At these borders, life adapts, blends, and innovates. The same is true within us.

At the edges of our capacity-when we face change, grief, uncertainty-we are called to stretch into new forms of strength. It is not ease that deepens resilience, but the meeting of tension with awareness.

Edges are not meant to break us; they are meant to reveal us.

They show us what we value, what we fear, what we are capable of when we stand between the known and the unknown. Each time we encounter an edge and return to our circle, we carry back wisdom.

Each time we stretch, our circle expands, and resilience deepens.

Holding Steady at the Edge

Resilience at the edge does not mean recklessness. It means presence.

It is the pause before reacting, the breath taken in uncertainty, the choice to meet discomfort with curiosity rather than panic.

At the edge, our nervous system may tighten, our thoughts may scatter-but when we remain steady, something shifts. We discover that edges are not walls; they are invitations to awareness.

Practices help us stay grounded at the edge:

- **Breath as anchor**: In moments of strain, the breath brings us back to center. It is the reminder that we are still here, still capable.
- **Naming emotions**: To say, *This is fear,* or *This is grief,* transforms the unknown into something recognizable, manageable.

- **Calling on support**: Edges are not solitary spaces. Resilience grows stronger when we lean on trusted companions, mentors, or communities.

The Expansion of the Circle

Every time we meet the edge with steadiness, the circle expands. What once felt unbearable becomes integrated.

The fear that silenced us becomes the story that strengthens us. The challenge that shook us becomes the lesson that guides us.

In this way, resilience is not static-it is alive, expanding with each encounter.

Think of a time when you faced a threshold: a loss, a change, a risk you did not want but could not avoid.

At first, the edge may have felt sharp, overwhelming. Yet over time, you adjusted. You found language for the silence, strength in the struggle, clarity in the unknown.

That experience did not erase vulnerability, but it expanded your circle. You are not the same person you were before-you carry more resilience, more depth, more capacity to meet life's next edge.

The Gift of Edges

The edges of our circles are not places to fear-they are places where resilience grows luminous.

They are reminders that life is not about remaining always safe within, nor about living always exposed without.

It is about rhythm: retreating inward for rest, moving outward for growth. The circle and its edges work together, one nurturing, the other stretching.

When we honor this rhythm, resilience grows naturally.

We stop demanding that we always be strong, and instead recognize that strength comes from movement-between protection and challenge, between sanctuary and edge.

In this balance, resilience does not feel like armor; it feels like a steady flame, one that burns brighter each time the winds rise.

So when you next find yourself at the edge of your circle, pause. Feel the threshold beneath your feet.

Remember that edges are not the end of safety but the beginning of resilience.

Step forward with presence, step back with wisdom, and trust that both movements are part of the same dance-the dance that keeps your circle alive, expanding, and whole.

CHAPTER 8

THE FORGOTTEN CROWN

Each of us is born with an invisible crown-not one made of jewels, but of dignity, worth, and inner authority. This crown does not glitter to the outside eye; it shines inward, reminding us that we carry within us the power to guide our own lives.

Yet, somewhere along the way, many of us forget it is there. We look outward for approval, for answers, for validation, and in doing so, the crown slips into shadow.

To remember it is to reclaim self-trust: the quiet authority that comes not from dominance, but from alignment with our own truth.

Self-trust is not loud. It does not need to announce itself, nor does it rely on comparison. It is the steady knowledge that

I can listen to myself. I can rely on my inner compass. I can walk my path with confidence, even when others do not see it yet.

This authority is quiet because it does not seek to control-it seeks to honor. It honors intuition, lived experience, and the wisdom that grows each time we meet life honestly.

The Roots of Self-Trust

Why do we lose sight of this crown? Often because we are taught to measure worth through external eyes.

From an early age, we learn to seek gold stars, applause, grades, promotions, approval. None of these are wrong, but when they become our only compass, the voice within grows faint.

Over time, we may begin to distrust our own instincts: deferring decisions, doubting feelings, questioning desires. The crown is not lost, but it is covered in layers of dust.

To rebuild self-trust, we return to small moments of listening.

We ask:

What do I feel right now? What choice aligns with my values? What does my body tell me in this situation?

Each time we honor these inner responses, we polish the crown, and its quiet shine begins to return.

Quiet Authority in Action

Quiet authority does not look like control over others; it looks like coherence within. A person grounded in self-trust does not need to argue loudly for their worth. Their presence communicates it. They make decisions with clarity, not haste.

They listen to feedback without losing themselves. They say yes with openness and no with respect. Their authority is not a performance; it is a steady current that others can sense.

Think of the friend who trusts their intuition in choosing a new path, even when others hesitate.

Or the colleague who remains calm in a heated meeting, speaking with clarity rather than force. Or the parent who raises children with both firmness and compassion, guided by their own values rather than every external opinion.

This is the forgotten crown in motion: quiet, steady, luminous.

Practices of Remembering

To remember the crown is to cultivate habits of trust:

- **Listening to intuition**: Notice the first gentle tug in your heart before the noise of logic or fear takes over. Often, intuition whispers truth before the mind rationalizes it away.

- **Honoring small decisions**: Self-trust grows not only in life's big choices but in daily ones. What do I want to eat? How do I wish to spend my morning? Each small honoring builds confidence in listening inward.
- **Keeping promises to yourself**: When you commit to rest, to a project, to a boundary-and then honor it-you strengthen your sense of reliability within.
- **Practicing stillness**: Silence and reflection create space to hear the inner voice that constant busyness drowns out.

The Ripple of Self-Trust

When we wear the crown of self-trust, others notice-not because it is displayed, but because it is embodied. Relationships shift; people sense our clarity and respond with respect.

Work transforms; decisions flow with integrity rather than confusion. Inner life deepens; we no longer chase every external sign of worth, because the crown within reminds us:

I am already whole.

Self-trust is not arrogance. It is not resistance to learning. It is the balance of openness and discernment, of receiving guidance yet knowing when to stand firm.

It is quiet authority because it requires no show, no noise. Its strength is in presence, in steadiness, in truth.

So place your hand gently on your head, if only in imagination. Feel the crown that has always been there. Let it remind you of your inherent dignity, your capacity to guide yourself, your quiet authority.

You do not need to shout to be sovereign in your own life. You need only to remember-and trust.

The Ash Beneath the Flame

Every crown has moments when it feels tarnished, hidden beneath layers of self-doubt. Even those who appear confident to the world often carry secret embers of uncertainty.

Doubt and low self-esteem are like ashes: they do not erase the fire within us, but they cover it, dimming its glow. To the eye, it may seem that the flame is gone, but beneath the surface, warmth still waits.

The hidden ashes do not signify weakness; they are reminders that the fire, though quieter, still exists, waiting to be stirred back to life.

These ashes often accumulate gradually.

A critical comment here, a failure remembered too often, a comparison that lingers too long. Each adds a thin layer over our flame until, one day, we look inward and wonder if the light is still there.

Doubt whispers that we are not enough, not ready, not worthy. Low self-esteem reinforces the whisper, telling us to shrink, to hide, to hand our crown to someone else. And yet, even in that silence, the fire is not extinguished-it is only waiting for breath.

How Doubt Finds Us

Doubt often arises at the edges of growth. When we are about to try something new, step into unfamiliar roles, or voice a hidden truth, doubt appears like a shadow.

It questions our worth: *Who are you to do this?*

It points to our scars: *Remember the times you stumbled?*

In these moments, it feels easier to withdraw. But it is important to recognize doubt not as truth, but as a companion of transition. Its presence signals that we are stretching, reaching toward new ground.

Low self-esteem, by contrast, can feel like the residue of years. It often comes not from a single moment but from repeated messages-subtle or direct-that told us we were less. A childhood of comparisons. A workplace that praised output but ignored humanity.

A relationship where our needs were dismissed. Each experience sprinkles ash on the flame until we internalize the dimness as identity. But this ash is not who we are. It is only what has settled on us, waiting to be cleared.

Clearing the Ashes

To clear these hidden ashes, we must first notice them. Journaling, reflection, or quiet honesty can bring awareness:

Where do I most doubt myself? When do I feel smallest?

Awareness is the first brush that moves the ash aside. Next comes gentleness. Harsh self-talk only adds more ash.

What clears it is compassion: speaking to ourselves as we would to someone we love.

You are learning. You are allowed to try. You are more than your mistakes.

Small acts of self-trust help reignite the flame. Each time we listen to our own intuition, honor a boundary, or acknowledge a strength, we fan the embers. Over time, the light grows, and the ashes fall away. It is not a single act but a steady practice-the daily tending of the fire.

Transforming Doubt into Depth

Doubt, when seen differently, can even serve us. It reminds us to prepare with care, to check alignment with our values, to stay humble as we grow.

Low self-esteem, too, can teach us compassion for others.

Those who have known the weight of ashes often become the gentlest encouragers, able to see hidden fires in others because they have searched for their own. In this way, the ashes are not wasted-they become part of the story of resilience.

Imagine standing again with your crown, its shine dimmed but not gone.

As you gently brush away the ashes, you see it was never destroyed.

It only needed remembering, polishing, restoring. Doubt and low self-esteem may return from time to time, but now you know they are not the crown itself. They are only the residue of experience, temporary layers on something eternal.

The Return of the Flame

When we clear the ashes, we rediscover not a louder, more flamboyant authority, but a quieter, steadier one. The crown shines again, reminding us: *Your worth was never lost. It was only hidden.* Doubt may still visit, but it no longer defines us. Low self-esteem may still whisper, but its voice no longer silences the truth. Beneath it all, the flame endures. And with each breath of self-compassion, each act of trust, it grows brighter, illuminating the path ahead.

The Endless Loop

There are moments when the mind feels like a hall of mirrors. Every decision, no matter how small, reflects back endless possibilities, each one demanding to be reconsidered. *Did I say the right thing? Should I have chosen differently? What if I was wrong?* This is the anxiety of second-guessing-a restless loop where the mind tries to outthink uncertainty. Though meant to protect us, it often leaves us drained, as though the crown of self-trust has slipped just out of reach.

Second-guessing is not a flaw of intelligence; it is the shadow of care. It arises when we want so deeply to do right, to be fair, to avoid harm, that we replay our choices until they lose clarity. Instead of anchoring us, this carefulness becomes a tide that pulls us away from our center. The crown feels heavy in these moments, as though our authority over our own life is questioned by the voice within.

Why We Second-Guess

Second-guessing often grows from the soil of past experiences. Perhaps mistakes once led to harsh criticism, teaching us to question every step.

Perhaps cultural or family expectations shaped us to seek perfection, to believe that worth comes only when choices are flawless. Or perhaps we carry the memory of being dismissed, and so we recheck our words, hoping not to feel that invisibility again.

Each of these experiences lays the foundation for the loop of doubt.

It also arises in moments of change. The unfamiliar invites the mind to prepare by imagining every outcome, every possible mistake.

What begins as preparation becomes overanalysis. Instead of stepping forward with trust, we circle endlessly at the threshold, unsure if we are ready. The anxiety here is not weakness-it is the mind's attempt to secure safety where none can be guaranteed.

The Cost of the Loop

The habit of second-guessing can leave us weary. Energy that could be used for creativity, connection, or rest is consumed by replaying the same scenarios.

Over time, decisions feel heavier than they are, as though even simple choices carry extraordinary risk. The self becomes entangled in constant questioning:

Am I good enough? Did I choose well? Can I trust myself?

The irony is that the more we question, the further we drift from the quiet authority that was ours all along.

Meeting the Loop with Gentle Authority

The way through is not to silence second-guessing with force but to meet it with gentleness. Begin with pause. When the loop begins, notice it: *I am second-guessing.* Naming the pattern loosens its grip. Then, breathe. A steady inhale and exhale grounds the body, reminding us that presence is stronger than spirals.

Next, ask: *What decision did I already make? What values guided it?* When we anchor our choices in values rather than in fear of mistakes, the need to replay them diminishes. For example, if you spoke with honesty, you can remind yourself: *I chose truth, and truth aligns with my values.* The outcome may vary, but the integrity of the choice stands.

Practices to Strengthen Trust

- **Limit the loop**: Give yourself a boundary of time-*I will consider this for fifteen minutes, then I will trust my choice.* Boundaries protect mental energy.
- **Affirm the crown**: Place a hand over your chest and remind yourself: *I am capable of guiding my life. I can learn from every step I take.* This physical gesture helps anchor trust.
- **Collect evidence**: Write down moments when your intuition guided you well, when your decisions led to growth, when you handled the unexpected with grace. Returning to these reminders helps rebuild trust in the self.

The Return of Quiet Authority

Second-guessing softens when we remember that no choice is final perfection. Life itself is a practice, an unfolding. Each step is information, each decision a brushstroke in the larger canvas.

To wear the forgotten crown is to know that authority does not mean never erring-it means walking with the confidence that whatever comes, we will meet it with honesty and resilience.

Imagine again the crown upon your head-not heavy, not dazzling, but steady.

Let it remind you that even when doubt whispers, even when choices feel uncertain, the quiet authority of self-trust is never gone. It waits for you to pause, to breathe, to listen inward, and to say:

This is my path, and I am enough to walk it.

The Gentle Path Back

Confidence is often imagined as a grand unveiling, a bold gesture, a triumphant return.

Yet in truth, it rarely arrives in dramatic moments. More often, it is reclaimed quietly, step by step, through the small choices that affirm who we are.

These choices may seem insignificant to others, but to the one making them, they are acts of sovereignty-reminders that the forgotten crown is still ours to wear.

Confidence is not a constant flame; it flickers. At times, it burns bright, guiding us through life with ease.

At other times, it dims, hidden under the ashes of doubt, criticism, or fatigue. When it fades, we need not search for a sudden spark. We can tend the fire gently, with kindling made of everyday decisions-each one a vote of trust in ourselves.

The Power of Smallness

Why small choices? Because they are within reach. They do not require radical transformation or flawless certainty. They require only presence.

Choosing to rise a little earlier to greet the morning light. Choosing to speak honestly in a small conversation. Choosing to rest when the body whispers for pause. Each of these is a statement:

I can listen to myself. I can honor my needs. I can guide my life in ways that matter.

Over time, these small affirmations gather strength.

They weave together, like threads forming fabric, until the cloth of confidence feels sturdy again. One act may feel modest, but repeated acts accumulate into quiet authority.

Everyday Acts of Reclamation

Confidence is reclaimed in:

- **Choosing authenticity**: Saying, *This is my preference,* even in simple matters, affirms the right to have a voice.
- **Keeping promises to yourself**: Whether finishing a task you committed to or honoring your need for rest, follow-through builds reliability within.

- **Allowing imperfection**: Choosing to act rather than endlessly delay for fear of flaw reminds you that progress matters more than perfection.
- **Celebrating small wins**: Noticing the courage in a conversation, the effort in a day's work, the kindness in your own actions reinforces your self-belief.

Each of these choices may seem like a drop of water, yet together they carve rivers. They restore the flow of trust that had once been interrupted.

The Circle of Self-Trust

Every small choice becomes part of a circle. The more you choose with awareness, the more trust grows. The more trust grows, the easier it becomes to choose again.

This circle is the foundation of confidence-not a sudden leap, but a spiral upward. It is like climbing a mountain through steady steps, each one small, yet each bringing you higher.

Importantly, these choices need not be perfect. Even when a decision does not turn out as hoped, the act of choosing itself builds confidence.

It proves that you are capable of moving forward, of learning, of adapting. In this way, even mistakes become part of the crown's polish, not its dimming.

Living the Crown in Daily Life

Reclaiming confidence through small choices changes how life feels in ordinary moments. The decision to pause before responding creates presence.

The decision to speak kindly to yourself in the mirror plants seeds of compassion. The decision to take a single step toward a dream-researching, writing, asking for help-ignites momentum. These are not grand gestures, yet they are deeply transformative.

Others may not notice these small acts, but you will feel their weight shift within you.

You will feel your posture straighten, your voice steady, your gaze soften with self-assurance. This is the crown remembered-not because it was handed back by the world, but because you placed it gently upon your own head again.

The Gift of Small Choices

Confidence does not demand grandeur.

It grows in the soil of small, steady decisions that honor the self. When you choose presence over avoidance, truth over silence, rest over depletion, creativity over fear, you are practicing sovereignty. You are saying:

I belong to myself. I can trust my choices. I can walk with dignity, one step at a time.

And so, reclaim your crown in the smallest of ways. With each gentle choice, you strengthen its shine.

With each step of trust, you remind yourself that confidence is not a performance-it is a practice. And in the quiet rhythm of daily decisions, you will discover that the authority you thought forgotten was never gone. It was waiting, patiently, for you to remember.

The Crown Within Reach

There comes a moment in every journey of healing when we realize the crown was never truly lost.

It may have slipped from awareness, it may have grown dim beneath ashes of doubt or the weight of second-guessing, but it has always remained near-waiting, patient, steady.

To wear the invisible crown again is not to become someone new, but to remember who we have always been.

It is not about grandeur or superiority, but about standing in quiet dignity, rooted in self-trust, aligned with authenticity.

This crown does not glitter with jewels; it glows with presence. It shines in the way you carry yourself when you know your worth, even if no one else affirms it.

It radiates through the steadiness of your choices, the clarity of your voice, the compassion in your heart. Wearing it again is not an act of claiming power over others-it is an act of claiming belonging within yourself.

The Ceremony of Return

Unlike a coronation with trumpets and fanfare, the return of the crown is often a ceremony of silence. It happens in the moment you choose honesty instead of pretense.

It happens when you trust your intuition over constant comparison. It happens when you rise from the ashes of doubt and say, *I am enough to meet this day.* Each of these moments is a quiet crowning, a placing of invisible authority upon your own head.

Think of the small rituals that affirm your sovereignty: writing in a journal to honor your inner voice, taking a walk to clear your thoughts, choosing rest without apology, speaking truth in a gentle tone.

Each act is a hand lifting the crown, each act a reminder that it belongs to you.

Living with the Crown

What does it mean to wear the crown daily? It does not mean perfection. It means living with alignment.

It means walking into a room without needing to shrink or expand to fit others' expectations. It means knowing when to say yes with full heart and when to say no with equal clarity. It means carrying compassion without losing boundaries, offering love without losing self.

The crown is invisible, but its presence is felt.

Others notice it not because you boast of it, but because your steadiness inspires trust.

They sense it in the way you listen deeply, in the way you hold your ground without aggression, in the way you move through life not with haste, but with presence.

The invisible crown turns authority into something luminous-quiet, steady, and deeply human.

Practices of Remembering

Wearing the crown again is a practice, not a single event. Each day offers opportunities to reaffirm it:

- **Begin with intention**: A simple morning affirmation-*I honor myself today*-sets the tone for carrying the crown.

- **Move with awareness**: Notice when you shrink, when you overextend, when you doubt. Gently adjust. Return to balance.
- **Speak from truth**: Let your words align with your inner compass, even if softly. The crown grows brighter each time you speak authentically.
- **End with gratitude**: At day's close, reflect on moments you trusted yourself, however small. These reflections are polish for the crown.

The Ripple of Sovereignty

When you wear your invisible crown again, the ripple extends outward. Children raised in its presence learn dignity without arrogance.

Friends feel safer being authentic in your company. Communities flourish when individuals carry themselves with respect, neither diminished nor inflated. The crown, though invisible, becomes contagious-reminding others of their own.

This is the quiet revolution of self-trust. It does not need banners or declarations.

It begins within, in the way you treat yourself, in the way you walk through each day.

And as more people remember their crowns, the collective shifts: a world less driven by fear of inadequacy, more guided by dignity, presence, and compassion.

Walking Forward

Now imagine yourself once more, standing tall, shoulders relaxed, breath steady.

Place the crown upon your head-not of gold or silver, but of light. Feel its weightless strength.

Feel how it aligns you with your center.

Know that it was never gone, only waiting for your return. Walk forward wearing it-not to be above others, but to walk beside them, sovereign in your own right, offering the example of quiet authority.

This is what it means to wear the invisible crown again: to move through life not as someone lost, but as someone remembered.

To honor the flame within, to polish the worth long hidden, to carry dignity not as armor but as light. And in that light, to meet the world-not with performance, but with presence; not with noise, but with truth.

CHAPTER 9

THE HUNGER WITHIN

There is a hunger that no meal satisfies-a quiet ache beneath the surface of achievement, a sense that something essential remains just beyond reach.

We chase fullness in many ways: through work, relationships, recognition, possessions, experiences.

Each pursuit brings a brief spark of satisfaction, yet soon after, the familiar emptiness returns. It is as if the heart keeps reaching for something it cannot name.

This hunger is not a flaw; it is part of being human. It is the echo of longing-the desire to feel complete, to belong, to live a life that feels deeply ours.

Yet somewhere along the way, we mistake *fullness* for accumulation.

We fill our days, our minds, our calendars, hoping that activity will silence the ache. But fullness does not come from more-it comes from meaning.

The Mirage of More

Modern life trains us to equate fullness with quantity. We are told that happiness lives in the next milestone, the next purchase, the next achievement.

This belief creates an endless horizon that keeps moving away as we approach it. The more we chase, the more distant contentment feels. Like drinking saltwater to quench thirst, the pursuit of "more" only deepens the craving.

We scroll through images of other lives, compare our journeys, measure our value against curated success.

Each glimpse leaves a trace of dissatisfaction-an unspoken question:

Why not me?

Yet beneath that question lies a misunderstanding. We assume that fullness is something external, something to acquire.

In truth, it is an inner alignment, a harmony between what we do and who we are.

Listening to the True Hunger

To transform this hunger, we must listen to it. Beneath every craving lies a need that is deeper and more tender. The desire for success may hide a longing for recognition.

The pursuit of love may hold a need for belonging. The obsession with productivity may veil a yearning for peace. When we pause to ask,

What am I truly hungry for?,

We begin to distinguish surface cravings from soul needs.

Try this reflection: The next time you feel restless, instead of reaching for distraction, place a hand on your heart and ask,

What is this feeling asking for?

Perhaps it seeks rest, expression, connection, or stillness. Often, the hunger that feels empty is not a lack of things, but a call for presence-a desire to return to ourselves.

The Art of Enoughness

Fullness is not found in excess but in enoughness. Enoughness is a quiet contentment that grows when we stop chasing and start receiving what is already here.

It is choosing appreciation over accumulation, savoring over striving. It is saying, *This moment, right now, is worthy of my attention.*

To cultivate enoughness, practice moments of intentional pause. Savor a meal without rushing. Listen fully in conversation. Watch the evening sky without reaching for your phone.

These moments do not fix emptiness; they reveal that it was never as deep as it seemed. Within presence, fullness quietly returns.

Rewriting the Meaning of Fullness

True fullness does not come from filling every corner of our lives; it comes from alignment. When our actions reflect our values, when our days echo our inner truth, the hunger softens.

We no longer seek constant stimulation because we are nourished by authenticity.

A simple life lived consciously can feel richer than a crowded one lived on autopilot.

Ask yourself:

Where do I feel most alive? What activities make time dissolve? Who around me brings peace rather than noise?

These answers are breadcrumbs leading back to genuine nourishment. The hunger within is not asking for more-it is asking for meaning, for depth, for a return to what feels real.

From Chasing to Receiving

When we shift from chasing to receiving, emptiness begins to heal. We stop demanding that the world fill us and start noticing how much it already offers.

Gratitude becomes the quiet companion that transforms hunger into wonder. The simple becomes sacred. The ordinary becomes enough.

Fullness, then, is not an achievement but a homecoming. It is the moment we realize that what we were seeking has been within us all along-a presence, a peace, a sense of belonging to ourselves.

The hunger was never against us; it was guiding us back to the table of authenticity, where what truly nourishes has been waiting all this time.

The Temptation of the Shortcut

When discomfort rises, the human heart instinctively seeks relief. We reach for what promises to soothe-an impulsive purchase, a scroll through glowing screens, another task to fill the silence.

These are the quick fixes, the momentary comforts that offer a spark of control. They work for a while. The ache quiets, the mind distracts, the heart steadies. Yet soon, the stillness returns, and the hunger beneath begins to stir again.

Quick fixes are not signs of weakness; they are reflections of our longing for ease. We live in a world that glorifies immediacy-where speed is mistaken for progress and distraction for healing. But the deeper currents of the soul move differently. They require slowness, patience, and gentleness. They ask not for bandages but for presence.

The Surface and the Depth

True healing is not an event; it is a process of meeting what lies beneath the surface. When we reach for quick solutions, we treat symptoms instead of roots.

A busy calendar may mask loneliness, but it cannot dissolve it. Reassurance from others may ease doubt, but it cannot build self-trust.

Even the most beautiful distractions-travel, success, relationships-cannot fill the spaces that call for stillness and reflection.

Healing asks us to descend into those quiet spaces. It invites us to listen to what the discomfort is trying to teach. Quick fixes tell us, *move faster.*

Healing whispers, *move inward.*

The Illusion of Immediate Relief

The comfort of the quick fix lies in its immediacy. The moment we act, we feel a shift-a rush of dopamine, a flicker of satisfaction.

It feels like progress. But the relief is often shallow, dissolving as soon as the next wave of discomfort arrives. This is because healing does not come from avoidance; it comes from acknowledgment.

The parts of us that ache are not asking for escape-they are asking to be heard.

When we chase constant relief, we unknowingly create dependency on the fix itself. The shopping, the scrolling, the performing, the pleasing-all become ways of managing emotion rather than transforming it.

Over time, this pattern deepens emptiness, because the root remains untouched. The hunger grows not from lack of effort, but from lack of depth.

The Courage of Slow Healing

Deep healing requires courage, because it asks us to sit with discomfort rather than rush past it.

It asks us to trust that beneath the ache lies wisdom. When we pause long enough to listen, we begin to understand:

The loneliness is calling for connection, not distraction; the fatigue is asking for rest, not stimulation; the sadness is yearning for expression, not suppression.

This slower path feels unfamiliar in a world of instant gratification, but it is the only one that lasts.

Like a wound that needs air to breathe, the soul heals when given space and honesty. Quick fixes close the surface too soon, trapping pain underneath.

True healing keeps it open long enough for light to reach it.

Practices for Deep Healing

To move from quick fixes to true healing, we begin by cultivating awareness.

- **Pause before reaching outward.** When the urge to escape arises, stop and breathe. Ask, *What am I truly seeking right now?* The answer often points toward a deeper need.
- **Allow the feeling to exist.** Sit with it for a few moments without judgment. Discomfort is not an enemy; it is a messenger.
- **Choose nourishment over numbing.** Instead of reaching for distraction, engage in something that restores-writing, walking, music, prayer, silence.

- **Seek depth in connection.** Share your truth with someone who listens with care. Speaking aloud what was hidden helps transform it.

These are not quick solutions, but living practices. They don't promise instant peace; they promise real peace, the kind that stays.

The Beauty of Patience

Patience is the quiet power that deep healing demands. It allows transformation to unfold at its natural rhythm.

In nature, a seed does not bloom overnight; it breaks open, roots downward before reaching for light.

Our own growth mirrors this. The parts of us that ache are also breaking open, rooting into wisdom before rising again.

To honor this process is to trust that nothing is wasted-not the waiting, not the silence, not even the setbacks. Each slow breath, each moment of choosing presence over escape, is a step toward wholeness. Healing asks us to trade immediacy for depth, urgency for understanding.

The Wholeness Beyond the Fix

When we release the need for instant solutions, we begin to feel differently. The hunger that once felt unbearable becomes a guide. The ache that once felt like weakness becomes a teacher.

We learn that healing is not about filling every void, but about finding peace within it.

Slow healing is not glamorous. It does not make noise. But it endures. It builds roots instead of rushes.

It leaves us with more than relief-it leaves us with wisdom, resilience, and a deepened capacity for joy.

The next time you feel the pull of a quick fix, pause and remember: beneath the urge is a call from within, asking not for distraction, but for devotion.

To answer that call is to begin the quiet, beautiful work of healing that lasts.

The Misunderstood Space

Solitude is often mistaken for loneliness, as though being alone means being abandoned.

Yet solitude, when chosen and understood, is one of the deepest forms of nourishment available to the soul. It is the space where noise settles, the heart finds rhythm, and the mind remembers its own voice.

While the world celebrates connection, solitude reminds us that connection begins within. It is not a void to be feared but a sanctuary to be tended-a quiet soil where roots of self-awareness, creativity, and peace can grow.

From a young age, we are conditioned to associate company with safety and silence with lack.

We fill our calendars and conversations to avoid stillness, fearing what we might hear in its depth. But solitude is not absence-it is presence.

It is the sacred pause where we return to our inner landscape and remember that our worth is not dependent on how many people witness it.

True nourishment begins when we learn to be with ourselves without restlessness.

The Weight of Constant Company

In modern life, we are rarely alone. The hum of technology, the stream of messages, the demand to stay visible-all these create a constant buzz that leaves little room for introspection.

Even moments of pause are filled with background noise: scrolling, chatting, consuming.

Yet beneath this constant company lies exhaustion. The hunger we feel after endless engagement is not for more connection, but for depth-for a reunion with our own thoughts, our own rhythm.

Without solitude, we lose touch with the inner compass that guides authentic living. We start absorbing the voices around us, mistaking their volume for truth.

Slowly, our decisions, desires, even emotions begin to mirror external noise. Solitude interrupts this cycle.

It clears the fog.

It allows us to hear what has long been whispering beneath the surface: the voice of intuition, of clarity, of self.

The Healing Nature of Solitude

Solitude heals because it gives us space to process. The emotions we suppress in busyness-grief, fatigue, confusion-find a place to unfold in quiet.

Sitting alone, we learn to listen to our emotions not as enemies but as messengers. The sadness that seemed overwhelming in crowds feels softer when met with gentleness in stillness.

The anxiety that spiraled in noise begins to slow its pace when given breath and attention. Healing requires stillness; solitude offers it.

In solitude, creativity awakens. The mind, freed from external demands, begins to play, imagine, and wonder.

Many of history's greatest thinkers, artists, and mystics drew strength from solitude-not as escape, but as communion.

They understood that solitude refills the well from which genuine contribution flows.

Without retreat, expression runs dry. Without silence, words lose meaning. Solitude is not withdrawal from life; it is preparation for deeper engagement with it.

Practicing Nourishing Solitude

To experience solitude as nourishment, intention matters. Solitude without awareness can turn to restlessness, but solitude with mindfulness becomes sacred.

Begin small:

- **Create pockets of quiet.** Ten minutes each morning before the world awakens can become a ritual of reconnection. Sit with tea, breathe, listen.
- **Leave space between interactions.** Instead of rushing from one conversation or task to another, allow pauses to digest experiences.
- **Step into nature.** Walk without music, without agenda. Let the rhythm of the earth remind you of your own.

- **Journal or reflect.** Writing in solitude transforms thoughts into clarity. It gives form to the unseen, structure to the inner voice.
- **Rest without distraction.** True rest is not scrolling or multitasking; it is being with yourself in peace.

These practices are not acts of withdrawal-they are acts of nourishment.

Through them, we learn that solitude does not isolate us; it prepares us to connect more deeply and authentically when we re-enter the world.

The Shift in Perception

When solitude changes from punishment to nourishment, something profound happens. We stop fearing our own company. We begin to savor it. The silence that once felt heavy turns into music. The time that once felt empty becomes fertile. We no longer use others to escape ourselves; we meet others from a place of fullness.

This shift transforms relationships. When we are comfortable in solitude, we no longer demand constant validation or reassurance.

We offer presence rather than dependence, listening rather than projecting. Solitude teaches us emotional independence-not detachment, but balance. It is the knowing that we can love deeply and still return home to ourselves.

The Gift of Being Alone, Together

Ironically, those who embrace solitude often connect more meaningfully. They bring to relationships a depth that cannot be found in constant interaction.

They listen without fear of silence, speak from reflection rather than reaction, and hold space for others without losing themselves.

Solitude, practiced well, becomes the foundation of empathy-it teaches us to sit with our own emotions so we can hold others' without resistance.

Returning to the Self

Solitude is nourishment because it restores our inner harmony. In its embrace, we remember what truly matters, what we truly feel, and who we truly are.

It strips away the excess and leaves us with essence. It reminds us that fullness is not found in constant motion, but in moments of still presence.

The next time you find yourself alone, resist the impulse to fill the space.

Instead, breathe. Look around. Notice the textures of silence-the hum of life, the rhythm of your breath, the beating of your own heart. In that quiet, you will find something quietly radiant: yourself.

And in that rediscovery, you will realize that solitude was never punishment-it was invitation. An invitation to come home, to refill, to remember that you are already whole.

When solitude becomes nourishment, the hunger within softens. We stop chasing fullness in others and start cultivating it within.

We realize that to be alone is not to be empty-it is to be in the most intimate company we will ever know.

The Modern Mirage

In a world that moves relentlessly forward, self-care has become a promise-a remedy for exhaustion, a celebration of individuality, a language of healing.

Yet somewhere along the way, the essence of self-care was diluted. What began as a sacred act of restoration often turns into another form of escape: a fleeting indulgence, a curated image, an attempt to fill emptiness rather than understand it.

True self-care and escape can look deceptively similar from the outside. The difference lies not in what we do, but in the intention behind it.

Escape whispers, *Run from the feeling.* True self-care says, *Sit with it, tend to it.* Escape numbs; self-care nourishes. One distracts the heart; the other listens to it.

The Allure of Distraction

We live in a culture that rewards distraction. When stress peaks, advertisements invite us to consume: spa days, scented candles, vacations, screens glowing with entertainment.

None of these are harmful on their own, yet when used to avoid our inner landscape, they become temporary shelters built on restless ground.

We feel momentary relief but return to the same exhaustion once the distraction fades. This cycle is not healing-it is postponement.

Escape thrives on avoidance. It allows us to ignore discomfort rather than understand it.

But healing requires engagement. The heart does not mend in noise; it mends in honesty. True self-care does not always feel light-it often begins with quiet courage, with the willingness to face what is tender, weary, or afraid within us.

The Essence of True Self-Care

True self-care is not about luxury; it is about alignment. It is not limited to rituals that please the senses-it is the deeper practice of honoring our needs with sincerity.

Sometimes, true self-care looks gentle: resting without guilt, taking a slow walk, reading a book that feeds the mind.

But at other times, it looks fierce: saying no, ending what drains the spirit, confronting truth, creating space for growth. It is not always beautiful, but it is always kind.

True self-care is not what we post; it is what we practice when no one is watching. It is the decision to turn off the noise and listen inward.

It is the discipline to maintain boundaries, to nourish the body, to protect the mind, to soften the heart. It is the understanding that care is not an event but a rhythm-a steady relationship with oneself.

Listening vs. Avoiding

To know whether we are caring for ourselves or escaping, we must listen to the body's language. After an act of escape, the mind feels distracted but the body remains tense.

After an act of true care, the body exhales-it feels lighter, calmer, grounded. Escape creates a temporary high; self-care creates quiet steadiness.

Ask yourself:

Does this soothe or numb me? Does this bring me closer to myself or pull me away?

The answers are gentle indicators. They help us discern whether our actions are rooted in awareness or avoidance.

True care deepens connection; escape distances it.

The Practice of Real Care

To transform self-care from escape into nourishment, intention is key. Begin with awareness:

- **Pause before action.** When the urge to escape arises, breathe. Ask, *What am I seeking right now?* Is it rest, reassurance, expression, or simply silence? Naming the need helps guide it toward true fulfillment.
- **Choose with consciousness.** There is nothing wrong with comfort. The difference lies in doing it mindfully. Watch the show, take the bath, sip the tea-but do it with presence, not as a means to disappear.
- **Integrate care into daily rhythm.** True care is not reserved for weekends or crises; it is woven into

every day. Sleep, nutrition, movement, meaningful conversation-all are acts of sustained self-respect.

- **Meet your emotions.** When sadness or frustration surfaces, resist the urge to bury it. Instead, sit beside it, as you would a friend. Write about it, breathe through it, allow it space. This is care in its most powerful form.

These simple acts shift self-care from external ritual to internal restoration. They remind us that care is not something we buy-it is something we build.

The Depth of Nourishment

When practiced authentically, self-care leads to renewal rather than escape. It nurtures resilience. It builds inner safety. It strengthens the ability to face life with clarity and grace. The one who practices true self-care does not run from life's storms-they rest within them, regathering strength until the winds pass.

True care also brings us closer to purpose. When we are rested and grounded, we see clearly what matters. We no longer fill time with noise but invest energy in meaning.

We choose connection over validation, peace over performance. We realize that taking care of ourselves is not selfish-it is the foundation of every form of love we can offer the world.

Relearning Rest

For many, the hardest part of true self-care is slowing down. The world equates worth with productivity, so rest can feel indulgent. But rest is not retreat-it is repair.

To rest is to allow life to recalibrate, to let energy and creativity flow back into alignment. When we rest intentionally, we stop chasing fullness through activity and begin to find it in being.

Create small rituals of rest. Light a candle not to escape, but to return. Sit by a window not to wait for distraction, but to witness light.

Let silence become your teacher, not your fear. These moments, though simple, rewire the nervous system, teaching it that safety and peace are available within.

The Return to Wholeness

The shift from escape to self-care marks the beginning of wholeness. We no longer run from pain; we learn to tend to it. We no longer chase comfort; we cultivate peace. The hunger that once sought satisfaction in quick relief transforms into nourishment through depth and presence.

True self-care is not an act of indulgence-it is an act of remembrance. It reminds us that we are not empty to be filled, but whole to be cared for.

When we begin to treat ourselves with this kind of reverence, the world around us begins to mirror it. We show up differently-calmer, clearer, more compassionate.

And that is the quiet power of real care: it heals not only the self but also the spaces we touch.

So the next time you reach for comfort, pause. Ask your heart what it truly needs.

If the answer feels grounding, it is care. If it feels numbing, it is escape. Both are human; one leads us home, the other delays arrival.

Choose the path that nourishes, and you will find that true self-care was never about retreat-it was always about return.

The Quiet Gift

There is a kind of joy that does not announce itself with fanfare. It arrives softly, like morning light filtering through curtains, like the first sip of tea after a long day.

This is the joy of simplicity-a joy that doesn't demand more, but invites us to notice what already is. In a world that celebrates excess, simplicity can feel like rebellion.

Yet it is within this quiet rebellion that the heart rediscovers its peace.

Simplicity is not about deprivation; it is about alignment. It is choosing depth over display, presence over performance. When we strip away the unnecessary, what remains is what matters.

In simplicity, we meet life without armor-unfiltered, genuine, enough.

The Noise of Too Much

Modern life teaches us to equate abundance with happiness. We accumulate-possessions, commitments, information, identities-believing that fullness lies in having more. Yet too much can dull the senses.

When every surface is cluttered, both physically and mentally, joy becomes harder to locate. We mistake stimulation for satisfaction, activity for aliveness.

Joy, however, thrives in clarity. Like light through clean glass, it passes most easily through simplicity.

When we quiet the noise-of comparison, of consumption, of constant doing-what remains is space: space for gratitude, for creativity, for breath. In that space, joy returns naturally, needing no invitation.

The Practice of Less

Simplicity is not a lifestyle trend; it is a practice of awareness. It begins by asking gentle questions:

What in my life feels heavy? What can I release without losing myself? What truly nourishes me?

Each answer guides us toward lightness. Simplifying does not mean removing beauty-it means curating it, allowing only what uplifts the spirit.

Start with the small and tangible. Clear a space on your desk. Unsubscribe from what no longer resonates. Spend an evening without screens.

Notice how even minor acts of release create ease in the body. The process of simplifying the outer world mirrors the inner one. As we declutter our surroundings, our thoughts follow suit. Stillness becomes easier to find.

Joy Hidden in the Ordinary

Simplicity reveals joy not by adding, but by uncovering. It teaches us that happiness often hides in plain sight-in gestures we overlook because we are rushing past them.

The warmth of sunlight on skin. The sound of rain against windows. The laughter shared in unguarded moments. These are not grand experiences, yet they fill the heart more completely than any luxury could.

When we begin to notice these moments, life changes texture. The mundane becomes magical, the ordinary sacred. Gratitude becomes effortless.

Each day offers quiet gifts: a familiar voice, a peaceful morning, a task completed with care. The more we notice, the richer our inner world becomes.

Joy is not a peak emotion to be chased; it is a steady hum beneath the surface, waiting to be heard when the noise subsides.

The Beauty of Slowness

Simplicity invites us to slow down-not to stop living, but to start living fully.

The pace of modern existence often fragments attention, scattering energy across countless tasks. Slowing down is an act of reclamation.

It allows us to inhabit moments completely. When we eat slowly, food tastes better. When we walk mindfully, the world reveals details we usually miss. When we speak and listen with presence, connection deepens.

This slowness is not laziness; it is reverence. It is honoring the rhythm of life rather than racing against it.

The slow life is not smaller-it is wider, richer, more felt. It opens us to a dimension of joy that speed obscures: the joy of simply being.

The Courage to Simplify

To choose simplicity requires courage. It asks us to step away from societal definitions of success and question what truly fulfills us.

It means saying no to what drains, even when it is popular. It means valuing quiet moments in a culture that equates worth with productivity.

This courage is not loud-it is steady, quiet, and deeply personal.

Simplicity also invites honesty. It reveals where we overcomplicate life to avoid discomfort, where we hold onto excess out of fear of emptiness.

When we face these truths gently, we realize that emptiness is not a threat-it is potential. Space is what allows new things to grow.

Living Simply, Loving Deeply

As simplicity settles in, relationships change. We begin to seek quality over quantity. Conversations become deeper, fewer words carry greater meaning.

Love becomes less about grand gestures and more about steady presence-the way someone listens, the way time feels easy together.

Simplicity in connection means showing up without pretense, offering the truth of who we are.

In this space, joy expands. There is no need to perform or impress. There is only the freedom to be.

The energy once spent maintaining appearances is redirected toward genuine care, toward creation, toward peace.

The Joy of Enough

At the heart of simplicity lies the realization that *enough* is a sacred word.

Enough is not settling-it is serenity. It is knowing that contentment is not found in accumulation but in appreciation. The joy of enough is the moment we look around and feel no lack.

It is the gentle exhale after long striving, the recognition that this moment, this breath, this life, holds what we need.

Practice the joy of enough each day. Pause to notice what already sustains you-the safety of your home, the meal before you, the people who care, the small victories that pass quietly.

Let gratitude weave through ordinary hours until you feel the fullness that simplicity brings.

Returning Home

Simplicity is not about doing less for the sake of less; it is about creating space for what truly matters. It is about coming home-to your body, your values, your joy.

It turns the hunger for more into an appreciation for being. When we rediscover joy in simplicity, the world feels softer. The days feel lighter. We no longer chase meaning-we live it.

So slow down. Breathe. Let go of what crowds your peace.

Look around-not for what is missing, but for what is already beautiful. The cup of tea, the shared silence, the sunlight through leaves-these are not small things.

They are reminders that joy was never lost. It was simply waiting for you to notice.

INTERLUDE II: HEALING MAP-THE CRACKS WHERE LIGHT ENTERS

Take a deep breath before beginning this interlude. Imagine the book pausing-not to teach, but to hold space.

This is your moment to reflect, to map the invisible paths of your healing. You have walked through storms, silence, and rediscovery. Now it is time to notice where the light has begun to enter.

The Map of Your Becoming

Close your eyes for a moment and picture a piece of pottery, once broken and now repaired with threads of gold. In Japanese art, this is called *kintsugi*-the art of golden mending.

Each crack, instead of being hidden, becomes part of the beauty, a record of resilience.

Your journey is no different. Every fracture in your story has let in a shimmer of light, a reminder that you were never ruined, only reshaped.

Now, open to a blank page. This is your map. Draw, write, or trace-whatever feels natural. There are no rules here, only reflections. Begin at the center with a circle: this is *you, now.* Around it, let the lines spread like rivers or roots. Along each branch, write or sketch the experiences that have shaped you. Do not label them as pain or triumph-simply as moments that mattered. You are charting not wounds, but wisdom.

The Cracks That Shine

For each place where something once felt broken, draw a line of light-gold, silver, or any color that feels alive. These are the cracks where resilience lives.

Maybe one line represents grief that taught you empathy. Another might symbolize loss that opened you to gratitude. A third might trace a moment when fear became courage.

Let your page fill with these radiant lines, like constellations of healing.

Pause often. Breathe. You are not fixing the past; you are illuminating it.

Each mark on your page is proof of your ability to mend, to grow, to transform. The cracks are not evidence of failure-they are evidence of endurance.

A Dialogue with Light

If words feel easier than images, write to yourself instead. Ask:

Where has the light entered me? What did I learn when everything became quiet? Which moments softened me instead of breaking me?

Let your answers flow without editing. You may find that the most tender memories hold the brightest light. Healing is not the absence of scars-it is learning to live with them as art.

The Art of Integration

When you finish, look at your map. Trace your finger along the golden lines, noticing how every path, even the difficult ones, leads back toward the center-toward you. This is integration: the understanding that everything you have lived belongs. Nothing has been wasted. Each experience, when held with compassion, contributes to the whole.

You might see that some cracks are still open, some lines unfinished.

That is beautiful, too. Healing is not a single moment; it is a living map that keeps expanding. The light will continue to find you in new ways.

The Invitation

Keep this map close-a visual reminder that resilience is not perfection, but participation. It is the choice to stay open to light, again and again. Whenever life feels heavy, return to this page. Add new threads of color, new words, new reflections. Watch how the design grows richer with time.

Your cracks are not your weakness. They are your openings. And through them, light will always find its way back to you.

PART IV

THE RETURNING

CHAPTER 10

MEETING THE STRANGER INSIDE

There comes a quiet hour in every inner journey when you begin to sense a presence that feels both familiar and foreign-a faint echo within you that you had forgotten how to hear.

It is the part of you that once dreamed freely, felt deeply, and trusted easily.

Somewhere along the winding paths of becoming, this part was left behind-not because you didn't care, but because life demanded survival over softness, pace over pause.

Yet here it is again, standing at the edge of your consciousness, waiting to be seen.

Reconciliation begins not with judgment, but with recognition. The abandoned self doesn't knock loudly; it whispers. It may show up as sudden nostalgia, an unexplained sadness, or a yearning you cannot name.

It speaks through fragments-a melody that once stirred your heart, a forgotten scent, an old photograph that pulls you inward. When you meet these stirrings, do not rush to define them.

Simply allow them to breathe. The self that was left behind is not lost; it is simply waiting for your permission to return home.

The Reunion of Wonder and Strength

The process of reconciling with this self is like meeting an old friend after years apart.

There is hesitation at first-a tender awkwardness. You might not recognize their face immediately, or remember the last conversation you had. But the soul remembers. Beneath the surface, there is an unbroken connection, a quiet trust that time could not erase.

The reunion happens not through words, but through presence-by simply being with what arises.

Sometimes, what you abandoned was not weakness, but wonder.

It was the version of you that believed in magic, that felt beauty without needing to own it, that laughed without checking who was watching.

Over the years, layers of practicality, fear, and expectation covered that openness. You learned to appear strong, to stay composed, to move forward without looking back.

But strength is not the absence of tenderness. True strength includes the courage to return-to turn inward and hold the parts that once felt too soft to survive.

Imagine sitting quietly with that inner stranger. Perhaps they carry the colors of your forgotten passions or the shape of your early innocence.

They might hold the stories you told yourself to stay safe, the tears you never allowed to fall. Listen to them. Ask gently:

What did you need when I turned away?

You may hear answers in sensations rather than words-a warmth in your chest, a heaviness in your throat, a sudden sense of peace. That is understanding taking root.

Reconciliation is not about repairing a broken identity; it is about remembering your wholeness.

The self is not linear-it is layered, cyclical, and infinite. The part you abandoned was never separate from you; it only stepped into shadow for a while, waiting for your light to find it again.

When you invite it back, you expand-you become more human, more real, more complete. In this gentle integration, the heart learns a new language-one that speaks through compassion rather than control.

The Art of Returning Home

There is humility in meeting the stranger inside. You realize that healing is not a performance but a quiet listening.

It requires patience-the kind that does not demand instant clarity. Sometimes, you will sit with silence, unsure of what it means. Sometimes, old emotions will rise like waves, unbidden and strong. Allow them.

They are not regressions; they are reunions. Each feeling is a messenger from the part of you that is learning to trust your presence again.

The world often celebrates becoming someone new-a constant reinvention. But reconciliation is different. It is the art of remembering what was already true.

You do not need to erase what came before; you only need to return to it with gentler eyes. Even your mistakes become sacred when viewed through understanding. Every wound becomes a doorway when met with awareness.

You begin to see that the stranger inside was never an enemy-only a mirror, showing you the places where love had not yet reached.

As you grow closer to this inner companion, you may notice subtle shifts. Your choices soften. Your relationships deepen.

The noise of comparison quiets. Life feels less like a series of tasks and more like a conversation-one between the visible and invisible within you.

You begin to act not from fear of loss, but from a sense of quiet belonging. This is what it means to come home to yourself.

And perhaps that is the essence of returning-not to who you were, but to the intimacy of being whole. The abandoned self does not ask for perfection; it asks for presence.

It does not need grand gestures; it needs honesty. When you meet it with open arms, something subtle but profound unfolds: the boundaries between your past and present begin to dissolve.

You recognize that you were never incomplete-only in transition.

In this reunion, life itself changes tone. Ordinary moments shimmer with new meaning-a cup of tea feels like companionship, a walk feels like dialogue, silence feels like music.

You discover that reconciliation is not an act you finish; it is a way of living-a constant softening toward yourself.

The stranger inside slowly becomes a friend, then a guide, and finally, a part of your every breath.

And from that place of inner reunion, something new begins to stir-a quiet curiosity about the future, not as escape, but as expression. Because once you have met the self you left behind, you no longer chase wholeness outside; you live it, gently, from within.

The Echo Beneath the Surface

Healing often begins in silence, but within that silence, old memories stir.

They rise not as intruders but as whispers from the depths, carrying fragments of moments you thought were forgotten.

A sound, a scent, or the way sunlight filters through the curtains-any of these can open a door to a memory that once lay dormant.

These recollections do not arrive by accident; they come when you are ready to see them differently. The mind recalls, but it is the heart that heals.

When memories resurface, they do not come to haunt; they come to harmonize.

They seek integration, not attention. Sometimes, they appear vivid and sharp, like a long-lost scene replaying in high clarity.

Other times, they drift in softly, half-formed yet familiar, carrying emotions that no longer belong to the present moment but still live within your body.

When they appear, your task is not to analyze them but to *receive* them. In allowing the past to speak, you grant yourself the freedom to listen with compassion rather than fear.

The Body Remembers What the Mind Forgets

Healing is rarely linear. The body stores what the mind cannot process, and when you slow down, those stored sensations begin to rise.

A tightness in your chest, a sudden tremor, a wave of warmth-these are not signs of weakness but signals of release.

The body does not lie; it reveals what was silenced. To heal is to let the body tell its story in its own rhythm.

When you allow it, you learn that the body's language is tenderness, not trauma-it longs to rejoin the narrative, to be seen and soothed.

You may find that some resurfacing memories are gentle-moments of joy you had overlooked in the rush of living.

Others may bring tears, but even those tears cleanse more than they wound. Healing asks for your willingness to sit in that middle space where memory and presence meet.

There, the pain transforms into perspective. The image that once brought ache now carries understanding. You begin to see that every memory, even the heavy ones, are threads in the tapestry of your becoming.

Rewriting the Inner Narrative

Every resurfacing memory is an invitation to rewrite the story you tell about yourself. Healing does not erase the past; it reframes it. When you hold an old moment with awareness, you change its meaning. The frightened child within you learns that they were never abandoned. The version of you that once felt unseen realizes they were always growing toward this moment of recognition. The power of memory lies not in what happened, but in how it lives within you now.

Try speaking to these memories as you would to an old friend:

What did you want me to remember?

Sometimes they answer through emotion, sometimes through quiet clarity. As you listen, something shifts-the grip of judgment loosens, and a sense of wholeness expands.

You begin to realize that remembering is not the same as reliving. It is reclaiming your truth with softer eyes.

Healing through memory is a sacred return. It is the process of reuniting all the scattered pages of your story and reading them with love.

No part of you is wasted; no experience is without purpose. The resurfacing of memory is life's way of reminding you that you are vast enough to hold it all-the pain, the beauty, the in-betweens. You are both the keeper and the creator of meaning.

And in that realization, something within you quiets. You no longer fear what may arise from the depths, because you trust yourself to meet it.

Memory becomes not a reminder of what was broken, but a map of how you've healed.

The once-forgotten moments become your companions, walking beside you-not as ghosts, but as guides, leading you deeper into presence, into peace, into the gentle knowing that every fragment has found its way home.

The Weight of Time Unseen

There are moments in every inner journey when you pause and look back-not to count achievements, but to feel the spaces where life seemed to pass without your full presence.

You remember the days that felt heavy, the seasons you drifted through, the years that blurred into survival.

The mind names them "lost," and in that naming, a quiet sorrow arises. Yet even in that ache lies an invitation-to see those years not as voids, but as veiled teachers.

When we think of time as something to be measured, we begin to see ourselves as behind or late, as if life were a race with invisible markers.

But healing does not obey clocks; it unfolds in its own rhythm, often in silence. The so-called lost years were not empty-they were gestation.

Beneath the surface of stillness, something essential was forming: resilience, depth, the subtle art of endurance. Just as seeds germinate in darkness, your spirit was growing roots in unseen soil.

Shadows That Ask to Be Heard

Depression is often misunderstood as absence, but it is more like saturation-the weight of unspoken emotion pressing toward expression.

In those dim stretches of life, you were not doing nothing; you were listening, even if you didn't realize it. The soul grows quietly in moments when the world cannot see its progress. What felt like paralysis was often protection, what seemed like emptiness was space being cleared for new awareness.

When guilt joins that reflection-when you tell yourself you wasted time, failed potential, or drifted too long-pause. Ask gently:

Who decided those years were wasted?

You may discover that your timeline was borrowed from others, shaped by comparison, expectation, and fear. True healing reclaims time from those illusions.

It invites you to measure not how far you've gone, but how deeply you've learned to stay-with yourself, your truth, your becoming.

The Quiet Redemption of Presence

Guilt thrives on distance-from self, from understanding, from tenderness.

The moment you turn toward it with compassion, it softens. You realize that the years you once called lost were filled with quiet lessons-lessons in humility, endurance, and sensitivity.

They taught you to listen for whispers beneath noise, to sense the small mercies hidden in stillness. Those seasons refined you, sanding away what was false so that truth could emerge bare and luminous.

Imagine sitting with your younger self from those years. They may appear tired, uncertain, or withdrawn. Do not rush to fix them; simply sit beside them. Ask:

What did you carry for me all this time?

You may feel their relief as you finally look with kindness instead of critique. In that gaze, guilt begins to dissolve-not because you erase the past, but because you honor its purpose.

Depression and guilt often come as twin mirrors, reflecting where love has yet to land.

They do not arrive to punish but to point-to the heart that longs for gentleness, to the part of you that wants to believe those years mattered. And they did.

The stillness taught you patience. The ache taught you empathy. The pause taught you presence. Healing, in its essence, is not reclaiming lost time but transforming your relationship with it.

Becoming Whole Beyond the Clock

As you soften into understanding, a quiet truth reveals itself: nothing lived with sincerity is wasted. Every breath, even the heavy ones, carried you here.

Time is not a straight line but a spiral-it circles back, revisiting what was left unseen, allowing deeper recognition each time. The lost years return, not as regret, but as wisdom folded within your cells.

They remind you that growth was never about constant motion, but about allowing stillness to teach.

When you stop measuring your worth by pace, guilt begins to loosen its hold.

You start to live from a deeper clock-the rhythm of being rather than doing. Each moment becomes an opening rather than a judgment. You begin to feel time as ally, not adversary.

And within that acceptance, the heaviness once called depression transforms into depth-a reservoir of feeling that gives color to your compassion.

So, when the thought arises-*I lost so many years*-you might instead whisper:

I was gathering myself.

Because even in silence, even in sorrow, you were becoming. The stranger inside-the one who walked through shadow-is not broken, but seasoned.

They carry the wisdom of endurance, the grace of slow unfolding. And when you meet them now, you recognize that every year, even the hidden ones, was part of your return home.

From here, the path widens-not away from the past, but through it. The so-called lost years become bridges, leading you gently toward the life that was waiting all along.

The Dawn Within

There comes a moment when the long journey of healing softens into a quiet, luminous joy-the joy of inner reunion.

It is not a loud celebration but a gentle unfolding, the kind that moves through you like morning light through mist.

You begin to sense that the self you searched for was never truly gone, only waiting behind the noise, patient and whole. When this realization dawns, a subtle warmth spreads through your being, as if every forgotten part of you is exhaling in relief.

The reunion with oneself is unlike any outer success or achievement.

It carries no trophies, no audience, no proof-only a deep, silent knowing that you have arrived. This arrival is not at a destination but into presence.

You no longer chase completion; you feel it.

The same eyes that once saw emptiness now recognize beauty in ordinary things. A quiet walk, a small kindness, a single breath-all become sacred moments of participation in life's wholeness.

Meeting the Heart's Reflection

The joy of inner reunion begins when resistance dissolves. For years, perhaps, you have searched outward for affirmation, trying to fix what you thought was missing.

Yet the heart never truly needed to be completed; it needed to be seen. When you meet yourself with honesty and compassion, the divide between who you are and who you thought you should be begins to blur.

You start to understand that the heart is not broken by experience-it is shaped by it, refined into empathy.

Imagine standing before an inner mirror and recognizing not the image you project, but the presence you have always carried.

There is tenderness in this seeing. You no longer demand perfection from yourself. You forgive your hesitations, your fears, your pauses.

You start to trust that even your detours were necessary paths, teaching you the texture of patience, the taste of surrender. The stranger within becomes a companion, and the dialogue between your inner and outer worlds turns harmonious.

This reunion brings a kind of humility-a surrender to the truth that nothing external could have restored you because you were never truly broken.

The cracks you once feared to show become constellations of wisdom, guiding you toward authenticity.

In realizing this, joy ceases to be an emotion; it becomes a quiet state of being, woven through your breath and gestures.

Living the Reunion

To live this joy is to move through the world with gentleness. You begin to listen more than you speak, to notice more than you judge.

The noise that once filled your thoughts fades into the background, replaced by an awareness that each moment is alive, vibrant, and new.

You feel the pulse of existence not as urgency but as rhythm. Life becomes less about fixing and more about flowing.

This is not an escape from the world but a deeper participation in it. The joy of inner reunion allows you to engage without losing yourself.

Relationships transform-not because they become perfect, but because you meet them from presence, not need. You listen differently, love differently, and even your silence carries understanding.

The world around you begins to mirror that inner peace; where you once saw distance, you now sense connection.

Try closing your eyes for a moment and feeling that connection inside your chest-the soft glow that asks for nothing and gives everything.

That is the essence of reunion: a meeting with the sacredness of your own aliveness. The heart, once guarded, now opens like a field after rain, lush and receptive. In this openness, gratitude blossoms effortlessly.

You find yourself thanking life for its patience, for the long detours, for every hidden blessing disguised as loss.

The Gentle Continuum

Inner reunion is not a single moment of enlightenment; it is a rhythm, a conversation that continues as you live.

Some days it hums softly in the background; on others, it floods your being with peace. But always, it reminds you that joy is not something to pursue-it is the natural fragrance of wholeness.

You do not need to hold onto it tightly; you need only remain open to its flow.

The more you live from this space, the more you see that nothing was ever wasted-not the silence, not the sorrow, not the waiting.

Each part of your story was preparing you for this harmony. And as you stand in that awareness, the world feels kinder, more intimate. Even time seems to bend around you, not as pressure but as presence.

The joy of inner reunion is the quiet knowing that you have come full circle-not back to who you were, but into the deeper truth of who you've always been.

It is the still point at the center of all your becoming, the heartbeat beneath every transformation.

And as this realization settles within you, it doesn't end the journey-it deepens it, leading gently toward the next unfolding, where wholeness continues to reveal itself, moment by moment, breath by breath.

The Quiet Practice of Being

To live with your authentic self is not a sudden awakening but a continuous practice-a gentle unfolding that deepens with each breath.

After the reunion with your inner being, life begins to reveal itself in new textures. You no longer wear masks to fit the rhythm of the world; you learn to move from your own pulse.

Authenticity is not rebellion; it is alignment. It is the art of honoring your truth without needing to prove it.

At first, this living feels delicate, like walking barefoot after years of armor.

The world may still pull you with its noise and expectations, but your awareness now knows the difference between outer motion and inner movement.

You begin to listen inwardly before responding outwardly. Every decision, even the small ones, becomes an act of self-respect. And with that, life grows quieter-not because there is less happening, but because there is more harmony between your inner and outer worlds.

Learning to Trust Your Rhythm

Authenticity is not a destination; it is a rhythm unique to your being. Some days it hums steadily, effortless and clear. On others, it wavers.

The learning lies not in maintaining perfection but in returning-again and again-to what feels true. There will be moments when you forget, when you slip into old habits of pleasing or pretending.

But now, you notice. And that noticing itself is awareness awakening.

To live authentically is to release comparison. You stop measuring your path by the pace of others. Instead, you honor the timing of your own unfolding.

Just as rivers find their course without rushing, your life flows best when it follows its natural current.

This trust births freedom-the quiet confidence that your way of being is enough, that your story need not mirror another's to hold meaning.

When you walk in this truth, your very presence becomes an offering of permission for others to do the same.

The Grace of Honest Expression

Living authentically also means learning to express without fear. The voice of your truth is not loud; it is clear. It speaks not to convince, but to reveal.

When you allow yourself to speak, create, or love from this space, there is no performance-only transmission.

What flows through you carries resonance because it is rooted in integrity. You begin to sense the difference between reaction and response, between effort and expression.

In conversation, you no longer rush to fill silence; you allow space for real connection.

In creation, you no longer strive to impress; you create to share essence. In love, you no longer seek to be understood first; you seek to understand.

These shifts may seem subtle, but they transform everything. You realize that authenticity is not about being transparent to the world-it is about being visible to yourself.

The Soft Boundaries of Integrity

As you live closer to your truth, boundaries emerge not as walls but as gentle lines of respect. You begin to say yes from sincerity and no from clarity.

You no longer confuse sacrifice with love or silence with peace. This discernment does not harden you; it centers you. You learn that it is possible to remain open-hearted while honoring your own space.

Boundaries built from awareness become acts of compassion-for both yourself and others. They create room for honest relationship, where connection is rooted in choice, not obligation. Living authentically invites you to stop shrinking to be accepted or expanding to be admired. You inhabit your natural size, the exact space you were always meant to fill.

Becoming at Home in Your Own Skin

Gradually, the self that once felt like a stranger becomes a home you trust. The noise of doubt quiets, replaced by a steady inner companionship.

You begin to feel comfortable in your pauses, confident in your simplicity, and content in your depth. Authentic living does not mean every moment is serene-it means you no longer abandon yourself when it is not.

In daily life, this authenticity expresses itself in small gestures: choosing silence over reaction, honesty over approval, presence over performance.

You no longer seek to control how life unfolds; instead, you participate with awareness. The outer world still shifts, but you move through it anchored in inner steadiness.

This is the quiet joy of living from truth-it requires no announcement, only embodiment.

The Living Continuum

The journey of authenticity does not end with self-discovery; it evolves with every breath.

Each day invites you to deepen the conversation between your being and the world-to live, not as who you should be, but as who you are becoming.

Some days you will walk with certainty; on others, you will return to listening. But through it all, you stay in dialogue with yourself, adjusting, softening, learning.

To live with your authentic self is to exist as a moving prayer-each act a gesture of presence, each breath a return to truth. You no longer chase alignment; you live it, quietly, in the rhythm of your choices.

And as you do, life begins to mirror your sincerity. Encounters feel more genuine, paths open with ease, and the once-fragmented parts of you move together in grace.

This is not an ending but a continuation-the unfolding of a life lived awake. From here, you carry forward not just the knowledge of who you are, but the lived experience of being it.

The stranger inside has become kin, and together, you walk into the world-whole, aware, and beautifully real.

Interlude II: Healing Map-*The Cracks Where Light Enters*

Take a deep breath before beginning this interlude. Imagine the book pausing-not to teach, but to hold space.

This is your moment to reflect, to map the invisible paths of your healing. You have walked through storms, silence, and rediscovery. Now it is time to notice where the light has begun to enter.

The Map of Your Becoming

Close your eyes for a moment and picture a piece of pottery, once broken and now repaired with threads of gold. In Japanese art, this is called *kintsugi*-the art of golden mending.

Each crack, instead of being hidden, becomes part of the beauty, a record of resilience.

Your journey is no different. Every fracture in your story has let in a shimmer of light, a reminder that you were never ruined, only reshaped.

Now, open to a blank page. This is your map. Draw, write, or trace-whatever feels natural. There are no rules here, only reflections. Begin at the center with a circle: this is *you, now*. Around it, let the lines spread like rivers or roots. Along each branch, write or sketch the experiences that have shaped you. Do not label them as pain or triumph-simply as moments that mattered. You are charting not wounds, but wisdom.

The Cracks That Shine

For each place where something once felt broken, draw a line of light-gold, silver, or any color that feels alive. These are the cracks where resilience lives.

Maybe one line represents grief that taught you empathy. Another might symbolize loss that opened you to gratitude. A third might trace a moment when fear became courage.

Let your page fill with these radiant lines, like constellations of healing.

Pause often. Breathe. You are not fixing the past; you are illuminating it.

Each mark on your page is proof of your ability to mend, to grow, to transform. The cracks are not evidence of failure-they are evidence of endurance.

A Dialogue with Light

If words feel easier than images, write to yourself instead. Ask:

Where has the light entered me? What did I learn when everything became quiet? Which moments softened me instead of breaking me?

Let your answers flow without editing. You may find that the most tender memories hold the brightest light. Healing is not the absence of scars-it is learning to live with them as art.

The Art of Integration

When you finish, look at your map. Trace your finger along the golden lines, noticing how every path, even the difficult ones, leads back toward the center-toward you. This is integration: the understanding that everything you have lived belongs. Nothing has been wasted. Each experience, when held with compassion, contributes to the whole.

You might see that some cracks are still open, some lines unfinished.

That is beautiful, too. Healing is not a single moment; it is a living map that keeps expanding. The light will continue to find you in new ways.

The Invitation

Keep this map close-a visual reminder that resilience is not perfection, but participation. It is the choice to stay open to light, again and again. Whenever life feels heavy, return to this page. Add new threads of color, new words, new reflections. Watch how the design grows richer with time.

Your cracks are not your weakness. They are your openings. And through them, light will always find its way back to you

CHAPTER 11

THE SPIRAL PATH

Healing, though often imagined as a steady climb upward, moves more like a spiral.

It circles and revisits, twists and expands, guiding you back through old emotions, familiar memories, and recurring lessons. Each return is not a failure but a deepening.

When you find yourself standing before the same feeling again, you are not in the same place-you are meeting it with new eyes, new gentleness, and a wider heart. The spiral does not move backward; it moves inward.

This realization dissolves the pressure to constantly move forward.

Healing is not about escape; it is about integration. You do not climb out of your pain but through it, layer by layer, understanding how every experience shaped your perception.

It teaches patience-the kind that allows you to see that what looks like repetition is actually refinement.

You are not looping endlessly; you are learning to move with awareness through the same rhythm at a higher octave.

The Dance Between Light and Shadow

Every true healing journey weaves light and shadow together. There are days when insight dawns brightly, and others when silence stretches wide.

Both are sacred. The moments of doubt or heaviness do not cancel your progress; they deepen it.

Shadow work is not a detour; it is part of the sacred choreography.

The heart cannot expand without meeting the places where it once contracted.

When light enters the dark corners of memory, it does not erase them; it illuminates their meaning.

This is how growth occurs-not by replacing pain with joy, but by allowing them to coexist until they form understanding.

Like night and dawn exchanging horizons, healing is a constant dance of contrast. It asks you to stay curious even when clarity fades, to trust that each descent prepares you for a higher ascent.

Meeting Yourself in Circles

The spiral path invites you to meet yourself again and again. Each cycle of healing reveals a new layer of the same truth-that you are whole even as you are becoming.

When old emotions rise, instead of asking,

Why am I here again? you begin to wonder, *What am I seeing differently this time?*

That shift in perspective changes everything. It transforms frustration into reverence.

Imagine walking through a forest path that loops around a mountain.

You may pass the same trees, the same stones, yet the view subtly changes with each turn. The light falls differently. The air carries new scents.

The landscape remains, but your perception has grown. This is how healing unfolds-the external story may repeat, but your inner understanding expands.

You begin to see patterns not as traps but as teachers.

In this awareness, you cultivate self-compassion. You stop measuring progress by how quickly pain disappears and start valuing how gently you meet it. The spiral invites softness.

It teaches that healing is not the absence of wounds but the presence of wisdom.

The Rhythm of Expansion

When you accept that healing is cyclical, the pressure to be “done” dissolves.

You realize that life itself is a series of openings and closings, inhalations and exhalations. Growth is not a permanent state but a living rhythm.

There will be seasons of clarity and seasons of quiet, times when you leap forward and times when you rest. None of these states are superior-they are all part of the natural cadence of becoming.

In the spiral, every pause carries purpose. What feels like stillness is integration-the body and soul absorbing what the mind has only begun to grasp.

This rhythm cannot be forced. Like tides returning to shore, healing moves in waves, and your only task is to listen. The more you honor this ebb and flow, the more peace you find in its movement.

Progress becomes less about reaching an end and more about deepening your presence within the process.

The Wisdom of the Spiral

Over time, you begin to see that the spiral path mirrors life itself-constantly unfolding, never repeating in quite the same way. The spiral does not trap you; it frees you from the illusion of linearity.

It shows that every experience, even the painful ones, carries you closer to the essence of your being.

The setbacks become signals of readiness, the pauses moments of recalibration, and the circles reminders that nothing truly begins or ends-everything transforms.

This understanding brings grace. You start to trust your rhythm, even when the path bends unexpectedly. You no longer rush healing, because you sense that every step, even the uncertain ones, belongs to the dance.

The spiral teaches surrender-not as giving up, but as giving in to life's intelligence. You stop asking when it will all make sense and begin to marvel at how it already does.

Living the Spiral

To live the spiral is to embody patience and wonder. It is to understand that your evolution is eternal, that each return is a deepening of love.

You meet your past selves with gratitude, not regret. You welcome the future without grasping for it. In the present, you find the center-a quiet still point from which everything expands.

From there, you live not in pursuit of healing but as its expression.

In moments when you feel yourself circling back, remember: the path is not punishing you; it is preparing you. What once felt like breakdowns are often breakthroughs unfolding in disguise.

Each cycle teaches you to live with more openness, more trust, more presence.

Healing, then, becomes less about mending and more about remembering-remembering that you are not walking in circles but spiraling home.

And so, the spiral continues-not as a test to pass but as a rhythm to dance with. Each turn brings you closer to your own center, where all beginnings meet and all endings dissolve.

From that place of quiet knowing, you carry the truth forward: healing is not a straight line; it is the sacred curve of becoming, drawing you again and again into deeper intimacy with your own life.

The Rhythm of Return

Healing is rarely a straight journey; it has its pauses, spirals, and occasional descents.

Just when you believe you have outgrown an old pain, it may resurface-quieter perhaps, but familiar. This return is not regression. It is the rhythm of healing calling you to witness your growth from a new vantage point.

Setbacks are not failures; they are reflections, gentle reminders that progress is not about perfection but presence.

When the old emotions rise again, it may feel as if you are slipping backward.

Yet, if you pause and look closely, you will see that you are not where you were. The feeling is the same, but *you* have changed.

You carry understanding, tools, and tenderness that you once didn't. A setback, then, becomes a test of integration-a way to practice what you have learned, not a sign that you have lost your way.

The Grace Hidden in Relapse

Relapse can be a humbling teacher. It strips away the illusion of control and invites you back into humility.

It asks, *Are you still listening to yourself?*

Healing is not about mastering your emotions but staying in relationship with them. When you revisit patterns you thought you had transcended, rather than reacting with frustration, you can approach with curiosity:

What is this moment trying to show me that I missed before?

Every relapse holds wisdom, often disguised as discomfort. It shows you where tenderness still needs to land, where boundaries ask for strengthening, or where your compassion can deepen.

What you call relapse is often the soul's way of fine-tuning awareness. It is the universe saying,

Let's revisit this-there's more to understand here.

When you respond with gentleness instead of guilt, the lesson unfolds naturally.

Meeting Yourself Without Judgment

One of the hardest yet most transformative parts of the healing spiral is learning to meet yourself in these revisitations without harshness.

The mind may insist that you've failed or undone your progress, but the heart knows otherwise. Growth cannot be measured in straight lines-it breathes, expands, and contracts like life itself.

To live authentically within the process, you must allow space for imperfection.

Try this: when you notice old habits returning, do not fight them immediately. Sit with them as you would with a visitor who has something important to say.

Ask softly,

What do you need me to hear right now?

Sometimes, what reappears is not the wound itself but the echo of unmet care. The very act of listening without resistance begins the release.

In these moments, forgiveness becomes a living practice. Forgiveness for not knowing sooner, for reacting instead of responding, for being human.

Every time you meet yourself with compassion, you build new pathways of trust within your being. The body relaxes, the heart opens, and what once felt like a setback becomes a renewal of relationship with yourself.

Lessons Beneath the Surface

Setbacks often carry messages hidden beneath their surface discomfort.

They ask you to slow down, to reassess, to realign. Perhaps they point out where you've been pushing too hard or neglecting your needs. Maybe they remind you that healing is not something you achieve-it's something you live.

In that sense, a relapse is not a disruption but a recalibration.

If you trace the pattern carefully, you may notice that each setback occurs when a deeper truth is ready to emerge. The lesson may not be visible immediately; it reveals itself slowly, like dawn unfolding.

Patience is essential. The spiral will bring you back to certain themes until they lose their charge, until understanding replaces resistance. When that happens, you begin to see how every return is also an evolution.

The Soft Power of Surrender

There is great power in surrendering to the natural rhythm of healing. Surrender does not mean giving up; it means letting go of the belief that you must always be in control of your growth.

It means trusting that even the pauses, even the returns, are carrying you forward. When you stop fighting the spiral and start dancing with it, life becomes gentler, more forgiving.

Surrender allows grace to enter.

It teaches you that healing is not an upward climb but a movement inward and outward, like the tide. Sometimes you advance by standing still.

Sometimes you progress by resting. When you allow yourself to move at the pace of your own becoming, you start to sense that the path itself is wise-that nothing is wasted, and everything serves.

Living the Lesson

The beauty of setbacks is that they remind you of your resilience. Every time you return from a difficult period, you carry more light, more clarity, more compassion.

You realize that you can be both the wound and the healer, both the question and the answer. The spiral path is generous-it allows endless opportunities to relearn love.

When you live the lesson, you no longer fear relapse. You welcome it as part of your rhythm, as an intimate teacher that keeps you grounded in truth.

Life will continue to rise and fall, to open and close, but your awareness will grow steady like a flame in wind.

And as you walk forward, you'll notice that the same moments that once felt like endings now feel like openings.

Because in the spiral, nothing is ever truly lost.

Every return holds a gift, every stumble leads to grace, and every lesson brings you closer to the center-the place where you finally realize that healing was never about reaching perfection, but about learning to love yourself through every turn of the path.

The Shadow of Familiar Fear

There comes a point in every healing journey when the past begins to whisper again-not to haunt, but to test the steadiness of your newfound awareness.

You may feel a quiet anxiety rise, a subtle tension that asks,

What if I fall into the same patterns again?

This fear is not a sign of weakness; it is the echo of memory trying to protect you. The mind remembers pain and wants to keep you safe.

Yet safety built on fear can become a binding if left unquestioned.

When old memories surface, they often bring the scent of familiar mistakes-choices made in haste, trust misplaced, words spoken or withheld.

The anxiety that follows is not proof that you are doomed to repeat the past; it is evidence that you are conscious enough to notice the pattern.

Awareness itself is the interruption. The fact that you can pause and ask the question means you are already standing in a different place within the spiral.

The Mirror of Memory

The mind is skilled at replaying what once hurt, as if preparing you for the same outcome.

It shows you images of old failures, reminding you of what went wrong, as though vigilance could prevent pain. But this rehearsal of fear does not protect-it drains.

To live authentically with your evolving self, you must learn to look at these memories not as warnings, but as mirrors. Each reflection says,

Here is where you once forgot your worth; here is where you can remember it again.

When anxiety arises, invite curiosity instead of avoidance. Ask gently,

What is this fear really trying to protect?

Often, beneath the surface, it is not the event itself that scares you, but the feeling of helplessness that once accompanied it. That emotion seeks your compassion now.

When you meet it with presence, the charge begins to fade. The past transforms from a threat into a teacher.

The Spiral of Awareness

The spiral path teaches that every return carries more light. Even when you revisit similar situations, you do so with greater clarity.

The same emotion may appear, but your relationship with it has changed.

You now recognize the early signs of imbalance-the tightening in your chest, the restless overthinking, the instinct to please or withdraw.

Where once you reacted unconsciously, you now pause and choose with intention.

That pause is sacred; it is the bridge between old habit and new freedom.

Instead of fearing that you will repeat the same mistake, remind yourself:

I am not the same person who made it.

You have walked through reflection, sorrow, forgiveness, and understanding. The version of you that stands here today carries the wisdom of all those lessons.

If the pattern returns, it is not to shame you but to show how far you have come. The spiral turns again, not to trap you, but to expand your awareness.

Turning Fear Into Guidance

Anxiety, when listened to with tenderness, becomes guidance. It points to the places that still crave reassurance.

When the fear of repeating old mistakes arises, it is often because part of you still doubts your readiness to live differently. Y

ou can soothe that part not by denial but by dialogue.

You might say, *I see your worry, but we are not who we were.*

We have learned. This inner conversation transforms fear from critic to ally.

Learning to live with this awareness means you walk with both confidence and humility. You understand that life may still test you, but tests are not punishments; they are opportunities for embodiment.

When similar experiences arise, you now have the chance to respond from truth rather than defense.

Each time you do, you reinforce trust within yourself-a quiet assurance that you can meet the world without abandoning your center.

The Art of Remembering Gently

Healing does not mean forgetting the past; it means remembering it differently. The memory of an old mistake need not be erased-it can become a compass.

When you look back through the lens of compassion, you see that what you once called a mistake was often a moment of limited awareness.

You were learning the language of boundaries, courage, or self-worth. The anxiety that surfaces now is not an enemy; it is an invitation to apply those lessons with grace.

Imagine holding your past self in your arms, whispering:

You did the best you could with what you knew then. Now, we know more.

This act of inner reassurance rewires the emotional memory. The body, which once associated action with danger, begins to associate it with safety.

Anxiety, in turn, softens into awareness. You begin to move through life not to avoid pain, but to live more consciously, more kindly.

Living the Spiral With Trust

To walk the spiral path with trust is to accept that learning never ends. The fear of repeating old mistakes gradually transforms into reverence for your evolution.

You stop expecting perfection and start embracing participation-a willingness to show up, knowing that even if missteps occur, they will become part of your wisdom.

What once triggered anxiety now sparks mindfulness.

This trust is not blind; it is embodied. It comes from having met your shadows and learned that they do not destroy you-they deepen you.

You carry forward with a gentle confidence that even when you stumble, you can return to alignment. The spiral ensures that no lesson is wasted; each cycle refines your clarity and strengthens your compassion.

So when anxiety whispers that you might fall again, you can smile softly and reply:

Even if I do, I will rise with more understanding.

Because healing was never about erasing the past, but about learning to walk with it-gracefully, consciously, and free.

The Illusion of Repetition

There are moments on the path of growth when it feels as though you are moving in circles.

The same patterns reappear, the same emotions resurface, and you wonder if anything has truly changed. Yet within that familiar feeling lies a hidden truth: progress often disguises itself as repetition.

What seems like returning to the same point is actually a deeper descent into understanding, a more refined version of awareness. The circle is not a trap; it is a mirror showing how much you have evolved.

Every time life brings you back to what you thought you had already healed, it offers a new lens.

You see what you could not before. The same situation unfolds, but your reaction softens, your perception widens, your compassion deepens.

This is the spiral nature of healing-each return carries more wisdom. To the mind, it may appear you are back where you started, but to the heart, you are arriving closer to truth.

The Spiral Beneath the Circle

The difference between the circle and the spiral is subtle yet profound.

A circle repeats; a spiral expands. The surface may look identical, but the movement is upward, inward, transformative. The mind, accustomed to linear progress, resists this shape.

It craves clear markers-before and after, success and failure. But healing speaks in rhythms, not milestones.

It weaves growth through experiences that feel repetitive until the lesson is fully embodied.

When you find yourself meeting the same challenge again, pause and ask:

What feels different this time?

Perhaps the pain lingers for a shorter time, or you can breathe through what once overwhelmed you. Perhaps you notice your own tenderness, or your ability to pause before reacting. These are the quiet signs of expansion.

Progress does not always roar; sometimes, it whispers.

The Quiet Architecture of Change

Growth is not always visible. It often takes place in the unseen spaces-between one breath and the next, between an impulse and a choice.

The outer circumstances might resemble the past, but your inner architecture has shifted. The foundations of awareness have strengthened; your emotional landscape has become more navigable.

Consider how rivers carve through rock.

The water appears to flow the same way day after day, yet each movement shapes the land beneath it. The transformation is slow but undeniable.

So it is with you. Each time you revisit an old pattern with more awareness, you carve new pathways within your being. Over time, what once felt like confinement becomes a channel for clarity.

Trusting the Rhythm of the Spiral

There is a certain grace in realizing that life repeats not to punish but to refine. The spiral moves in its own rhythm, looping through lessons with patience.

The deeper your trust in this process, the less urgency you feel to arrive anywhere. You stop chasing resolution and start embracing revelation.

What once felt like stagnation becomes sacred practice-a rehearsal for consciousness.

You might notice that relationships, situations, or emotions seem to cycle through familiar patterns. But this time, you respond differently.

You speak truth where you once stayed silent. You choose gentleness where you once defended. You recognize that progress is not about escaping repetition but about inhabiting it with greater wisdom.

This awareness turns what felt like circles into living proof of growth.

The Gift Hidden in the Loop

Each return to a familiar pattern brings with it a hidden gift-the chance to see your evolution in motion. The very act of noticing that you have been here before means you are no longer lost inside it.

Awareness lifts you above the loop, allowing you to witness it with compassion instead of confusion. You begin to thank these moments for their persistence.

They are life's way of ensuring that your lessons are not just learned but lived.

When you meet an old emotion, instead of frustration, you might whisper gratitude:

You came back so I could meet you differently.

This simple shift transforms repetition into realization. The circle becomes a sanctuary for reflection rather than a prison of the past.

You see that growth has been happening quietly all along, in the spaces between your efforts and your surrender.

Living the Spiral of Becoming

To live the spiral is to accept that mastery is not a straight ascent but a dance of return.

Each turn of the path brings you closer to your essence, polishing your awareness through contact with the familiar. You stop asking,

When will this end? and start wondering,

What more can this teach me?

That question opens the heart.

As you walk this path, you begin to sense that progress is not about reaching a new destination but about deepening your intimacy with life.

The same emotions that once unsettled you now guide you toward wholeness.

The same mistakes now appear as markers of growth. Even the moments that feel like stillness shimmer with movement beneath the surface.

The circle becomes a spiral, and the spiral becomes home.

You realize that healing was never about escape-it was always about embodiment. The spiral does not pull you away from yourself; it draws you closer to the center, where awareness resides.

From that center, you can look upon your journey and see that every loop was love's way of teaching you how to live in harmony with your becoming.

And as the spiral turns again, you recognize the beauty of its design. Nothing was ever wasted.

Every return was progress in disguise-an invitation to meet yourself anew, to walk familiar ground with a lighter step, and to know that even when the path curves back, you are still moving forward, deeper into the art of being whole.

The Gentle Art of Surrender

Healing, at its essence, asks for trust-a willingness to walk through the unseen and believe that each step, even when uncertain, carries you closer to wholeness.

The process of return is not about going back to who you were; it is about deepening into who you are becoming. Trust is the thread that weaves all moments together-the joy, the pauses, the unraveling, and the rebuilding.

Without it, the spiral feels chaotic. With it, every curve becomes meaningful.

Surrender is not weakness; it is wisdom. It is the quiet knowing that you do not need to control the rhythm of your growth. The spiral moves with its own intelligence, revisiting, refining, and revealing in divine timing.

When you stop resisting where the path leads, you begin to sense an invisible hand guiding you-through the messiness, through the mystery, toward the center that has always been home.

The Return as Renewal

Returning is often misunderstood as regression. Yet in the language of healing, to return is to renew.

Each time you circle back to an old emotion, you meet it with more maturity, more compassion.

The spiral does not take you backward; it invites you deeper. It brings you face-to-face with what was left unfinished, not to shame you, but to complete the cycle with gentleness.

The process of return is sacred. It honors the truth that growth is not about constant ascent but rhythmic expansion. You fall, you rise, you pause-each motion part of the same divine choreography.

When you begin to trust this rhythm, fear loosens its grip. You stop asking,

Why am I here again? and begin to wonder, *What new wisdom is waiting for me this time?*

In that shift, frustration softens into reverence.

The Language of Life's Timing

Trusting the process means learning to speak the language of timing-the pauses, the delays, the detours. The spiral path teaches that nothing truly arrives late.

Even the moments that feel like stagnation are gestation, preparing you for the next unfolding.

When you can rest inside uncertainty without rushing to fix it, you begin to live from faith rather than fear.

There are seasons when life asks for action, and others when it asks for stillness. Both are progress.

Trusting the process means you no longer measure yourself by speed or visible achievement, but by presence. You start to sense that life has an intelligence far greater than your plans.

The detour was never a deviation; it was direction disguised as delay.

The Center That Never Leaves You

In the spiral, there is a point that never moves-the still center around which everything turns. When you trust the process of return, you learn to anchor yourself in that center.

It is the awareness beneath every emotion, the silence beneath every story. Even when you feel lost, this center remains untouched, patient, and luminous.

It is the essence of who you are-the observer, the witness, the soul.

When the mind races or the heart trembles, pause and breathe into this stillness.

Feel it holding you even as life swirls around. The center does not demand belief; it reveals itself through experience. The more you return to it, the less you fear the spiral's motion.

You begin to understand that the return is not a detour away from your path-it *is* the path.

The Alchemy of Trust

Trust transforms how you experience the unknown. It turns anxiety into curiosity, resistance into acceptance, and confusion into clarity.

To trust is to allow life to unfold without demanding immediate understanding. It is to hold uncertainty as sacred, knowing that the unseen parts of your journey are working in your favor.

Each time you surrender control, you create space for grace.

Think of trust as an inner alchemy-a slow turning of fear into faith.

You practice it in small ways: choosing patience over panic, gratitude over judgment, presence over prediction. Gradually, this practice reshapes your relationship with life. You begin to see that every return, even the unexpected ones, carries a hidden alignment.

What once felt like repetition now feels like refinement.

Living the Return

To live the process of return is to move through life with open hands.

It is to meet each moment not with demand, but with devotion. You no longer rush to escape discomfort; you listen to it. You no longer chase joy; you cultivate it quietly within.

Every time you circle back to an old emotion, you bring more awareness, more light, more love.

This is the essence of trust-a deep, embodied faith that the spiral knows the way.

Even when you cannot see the next turn, you sense that it leads you exactly where you are meant to go. The path becomes less about effort and more about allowance.

You realize that trusting the process is not passive; it is profoundly active. It is an ongoing dance with the unseen intelligence that animates all of life.

The Grace of Belonging

When you fully trust the process of return, you feel an unexpected peace-a sense of belonging not just to the joyful moments but to the uncertain ones too.

You start to see beauty in the pauses, meaning in the meanders, purpose in the returns.

You live with an inner confidence that nothing is wasted, that every step has its place in the choreography of becoming.

From this trust, gratitude blossoms naturally. You thank the spiral for its patience, for the way it circles you closer to truth with each turn.

And as you walk, you realize that trusting the process of return is not about knowing where you are going, but remembering who walks within you-the constant, luminous self that has never once left your side.

CHAPTER 12

THE STRENGTH OF GENTLE HANDS

For much of life, we are taught that strength means resistance-holding firm, staying unmoved, standing tall against the storm.

Yet the deeper truth reveals itself slowly: strength is not the absence of softness but the ability to remain open amid uncertainty.

Real strength is not in the armor but in the heart that dares to feel beneath it. Compassion, then, is strength in its purest form-a power that transforms without force, heals without demand, and connects without condition.

To redefine strength as compassion is to challenge the old narratives that glorify hardness.

It means understanding that the most enduring power is not control but care, not dominance but understanding. Gentleness is not fragility; it is deliberate grace.

It takes immense courage to meet the world without closing off, to hold tenderness in a world that often rewards detachment.

The gentle hands are not weak-they are steady, aware, and alive.

The Courage to Feel

Compassion asks you to feel deeply-for yourself, for others, for life itself. It asks you to stay present when discomfort arises, to resist the impulse to turn away.

This kind of courage is quiet but profound. It is easier to harden, to dismiss, to distance. But the brave choice is to remain open, to allow the current of emotion to pass through without resistance. Strength lives in that openness.

When you allow yourself to feel, you begin to understand that emotions are not enemies but messengers. Anger may point to injustice, sadness to loss, fear to love.

Compassion gives you the capacity to listen to these voices without judgment. You hold them as you would hold a fragile bird-not to binding it, but to comfort it.

The heart grows strong not by avoidance, but by tenderness.

The Alchemy of Understanding

Compassion is not a single act; it is a way of seeing. It is the art of recognizing the shared humanity that lives beneath all behavior.

To see someone through compassionate eyes is to understand that every action-even the misguided ones-springs from an unmet need, a forgotten wound, or a moment of confusion.

This recognition does not excuse harm but transforms the way you meet it. Instead of reacting with bitterness, you respond with clarity and care.

This is the alchemy of compassion: it turns judgment into understanding, pain into presence.

When you practice this in your daily life-in your conversations, in your silences, in the way you hold your own mistakes-you begin to sense a deeper strength rising within you.

It is not the kind of strength that shouts or conquers. It is the kind that heals and harmonizes.

The Strength of Self-Compassion

Often, the hardest person to extend compassion to is yourself. We are taught to offer kindness outwardly, yet we speak harshly to our own hearts. Redefining strength begins here-by softening the inner dialogue.

To hold yourself gently is not indulgence; it is integrity. It acknowledges that growth cannot flourish under criticism, only under care.

When you make a mistake, when you falter or fall short, compassion becomes your hand reaching inward.

It says, *I see you learning.*

It invites patience into the places where pressure once lived. Over time, self-compassion becomes the soil from which authentic strength grows.

You stop striving to prove your worth and begin to trust in your inherent value. The more gently you treat yourself, the more courage you have to meet the world with openness.

The Balance of Boundaries and Empathy

To live compassionately does not mean allowing everything. True compassion includes discernment. It understands that saying no can also be an act of love-for yourself and for others.

Boundaries built from compassion are not walls; they are rivers guiding connection in healthy directions.

They protect your peace while preserving your capacity to care.

When compassion and strength dance together, empathy no longer drains you; it replenishes you. You give without losing yourself, listen without absorbing pain, and love without fear of depletion.

This balance creates a quiet confidence-a knowing that you can face whatever comes without closing your heart.

You learn that gentleness can coexist with firmness, and that saying yes to your truth sometimes means saying no elsewhere.

The Ripple of Gentle Presence

Strength expressed through compassion radiates outward. It shifts rooms, softens conversations, and opens pathways where confrontation once stood.

When you move through life with gentle hands-hands that hold rather than grip, that soothe rather than strike-you become a mirror for others to rediscover their own softness.

Your calm presence reminds them that vulnerability is not a flaw but a doorway to connection.

Compassion is contagious. When you offer it, you give others permission to exhale, to drop their defenses, to meet you with sincerity.

In this way, compassion becomes a quiet revolution-not loud or forceful, but deeply transformative. It changes the texture of interaction, the atmosphere of relationships, the tone of communities.

It reminds humanity of its shared pulse.

Living as Gentle Strength

Redefining strength as compassion is not a one-time realization; it is a lifelong practice.

It means showing up each day with the intention to understand before reacting, to heal rather than harden. Some days it will feel effortless; other days it will require conscious effort.

But with each choice to lead with compassion, you rewrite the narrative of strength itself.

Living this way transforms your perception of power. You realize that the truest form of influence lies not in control but in presence-in the way you make others feel seen, heard, and valued.

You begin to understand that gentleness is not the absence of strength but its highest expression. And in that realization, your hands-once clenched in defense-open naturally, ready to create, to comfort, to hold.

As the spiral of growth continues, compassion becomes both your compass and your courage.

It guides you back to your center when life feels scattered, reminding you that strength has never been about being unbreakable-it has always been about remaining open.

The gentle hands, steady and sure, carry the world not through force, but through love.

The Quiet Rebellion of Softness

To be gentle in a harsh world is an act of quiet rebellion. It is to hold grace where bitterness could grow, to offer warmth where indifference prevails. Gentleness is not the denial of pain but the refusal to let it harden you.

In a world that glorifies speed, competition, and control, choosing tenderness becomes a revolutionary form of strength. It is not about turning away from reality but meeting it with a deeper kind of courage-one that transforms rather than resists.

When the world feels loud and unkind, gentleness becomes your way of saying:

I will not add to the noise.

It becomes a conscious decision to pause before reacting, to listen before speaking, to extend understanding before judgment. This does not mean allowing cruelty or ignoring injustice; rather, it means acting with integrity and awareness.

Gentleness does not make you passive-it makes you precise. It channels energy with intention, not aggression.

The Strength Hidden in Soft Hands

Gentleness is often misunderstood as fragility, yet it takes immense inner stability to remain kind in an environment that challenges your peace.

The gentle hands do not shake because they are weak-they are steady because they are anchored in understanding. It takes strength to stay calm when provoked, to offer kindness when dismissed, and to stay open when the world suggests you close.

The power of gentleness lies in its quiet persistence.

It does not demand recognition; it simply continues to care. Like water shaping stone, it works slowly but surely, carving beauty into the hardest surfaces.

The gentle spirit is not naïve-it is wise enough to know that true change does not always come through force, but through presence, patience, and unwavering authenticity.

Meeting Harshness Without Becoming It

Gentleness does not mean you are untouched by harshness. You feel deeply-perhaps more than most-but you learn to transmute what you feel rather than replicate it.

When someone speaks with cruelty, you do not mirror their tone; you ground yourself in awareness and choose a higher response. This is not weakness; it is mastery. You refuse to let the outside world dictate the quality of your inner one.

To live gently in a harsh world is to cultivate inner balance. It is to remind yourself that peace is not the absence of challenge but the presence of choice.

When you meet cruelty with compassion, indifference with care, you break the cycle that perpetuates suffering.

You become the interruption-the still point in a world that spins too fast. Gentleness, in this way, is both shield and offering.

The Practice of Gentle Boundaries

Living gently does not mean being endlessly available or self-sacrificing.

Gentleness thrives within boundaries. It knows when to step back, when to rest, when to say no with grace. True gentleness respects both self and other.

It understands that giving from depletion creates distortion, while giving from wholeness creates harmony.

Practicing gentle boundaries means recognizing that you can care deeply without carrying everything. It is allowing yourself to be compassionate without being consumed.

This balance protects your softness, ensuring that it remains a source of strength rather than exhaustion. In this way, boundaries are not barriers-they are the structure that keeps your tenderness alive.

The Language of Presence

Gentleness communicates without words. It is felt in the tone of your voice, the patience in your gaze, the way you listen without interruption.

In a world full of distraction, your full presence becomes an act of love. When you give someone your attention-undivided, unhurried-you remind them that they matter. That, in itself, is healing.

Even silence can be gentle. The quiet between words can carry more warmth than explanation. Presence is the language of gentleness because it asks for nothing but awareness.

It does not rush to fix or correct-it simply *is*. And in that being, something shifts. Others begin to soften too. The world, harsh as it may seem, responds to gentleness like the earth responds to rain-slowly, silently, and inevitably.

The Resilience of a Gentle Heart

Gentleness and resilience are not opposites-they are companions. The gentle heart feels deeply and still chooses to love.

It bends but does not break, because its strength lies in flexibility, not rigidity. It knows that storms will pass, that pain transforms, and that compassion is not a luxury but a necessity.

Resilience through gentleness means allowing yourself to recover without rushing.

It means trusting that healing does not always roar-sometimes it whispers. You rebuild not by force but by faith, knowing that every small act of kindness, every moment of tenderness, reshapes the world in subtle yet powerful ways.

Gentleness becomes both the process and the product of true strength.

Living the Way of Gentle Power

To live gently in a harsh world is to walk with intention. It is to understand that every encounter offers a choice-to react or to respond, to close or to open, to hurt or to heal.

Gentleness does not deny reality; it redefines your relationship with it. It allows you to move through the world without being consumed by it.

You learn that softness is not the opposite of power-it is its refinement.

The gentle hands hold space where others grip tightly. They heal by touch, by word, by presence. They remind the world that love is not naïve-it is necessary.

When you embody gentleness, you become a quiet force of restoration. You make it possible for others to breathe again.

And as the world continues to turn, your gentleness becomes your compass-steady, unwavering, real. It does not shield you from life; it guides you through it.

The strength of gentle hands lies not in their ability to resist the storm, but in their willingness to reach through it-offering warmth, offering peace, offering proof that kindness can still thrive, even here.

The Invisible Medicine of Connection

Kindness is the language that bridges hearts when words fall short. It is the quiet medicine that mends unseen wounds, restoring trust where distance has grown.

In a world often marked by hurry and noise, kindness acts as a gentle pause-a reminder that we are, at our core, built to care for one another.

Every small act of kindness-a smile, a soft word, a moment of genuine listening-ripples far beyond its moment, altering the energy of a space, softening what once felt divided.

Relationships, whether between two people or within entire communities, thrive not on perfection but on presence.

When kindness enters the exchange, it turns tension into understanding, defensiveness into openness.

It says, *I see you; I care enough to meet you where you are.*

Healing begins here-in that simple recognition of shared humanity.

The Healing Touch of Everyday Gestures

Kindness is rarely grand or theatrical. It lives in the ordinary-in the way you choose patience over reaction, in the way you remember a name, in the way you check in on someone quietly.

These gestures may seem small, but their cumulative effect is profound. They signal safety. They rebuild bridges worn down by misunderstanding.

In relationships, kindness acts as both balm and bridge-it soothes the ache and reconnects what conflict tried to separate.

When you practice kindness, you give others permission to soften too. It creates an atmosphere where honesty can breathe, where vulnerability feels safe enough to emerge.

Often, healing does not require resolution; it requires presence. Kindness becomes that steady presence-the soft ground where forgiveness can root itself.

Kindness as the Language of Listening

True kindness listens before it speaks. It does not rush to fix or advise; it listens to understand.

To listen with kindness is to give someone the rare gift of being seen without judgment. It requires patience-the willingness to hold space without agenda. In a relationship, this kind of listening has the power to dissolve years of distance. People begin to trust again when they feel truly heard.

Communities, too, begin to heal through this kind of listening. When conversations move from debate to dialogue, from opinion to empathy, the collective heart begins to open.

Kindness changes the tone of interaction. It reminds people that being right is not as important as being connected. It turns coexistence into community.

The Ripple Effect of Gentle Leadership

Kindness is not passive; it is profoundly influential. A single act of compassion can shift an entire environment. Leaders who embody kindness create cultures of trust and collaboration.

They show that respect and care can coexist with excellence and accountability. When kindness is modeled at the top, it flows through every interaction beneath it-from teams to neighborhoods, from families to societies.

In communities, kindness acts like sunlight through clouds-quietly persistent, warming even the coldest corners. It inspires generosity, cooperation, and shared purpose.

When people feel cared for, they begin to care for others. This reciprocity is how communities heal-not through grand programs or systems alone, but through consistent, genuine acts of compassion that remind everyone they belong.

The Courage to Be Kind

Kindness takes courage, especially when the world feels fragmented or cynical. It requires vulnerability-a willingness to extend care without guarantee of return. Yet this courage is what gives kindness its transformative power.

To choose gentleness in the face of misunderstanding is to hold light where darkness expects defeat.

When you offer kindness to someone who is hurting or angry, you interrupt the cycle of reaction.

You become a mirror that reflects back possibility-the chance that connection is still worth trying.

This does not mean tolerating harm; it means standing firm in your values while keeping your heart open. It means realizing that kindness and boundaries can exist in the same breath-that compassion can be both soft and strong.

The Alchemy of Mutual Healing

One of the quiet miracles of kindness is that it heals both giver and receiver. When you act with compassion, your own heart expands. The act of giving warmth creates warmth within.

Neuroscientists have found what sages have long known: kindness releases oxytocin, the hormone of connection, easing stress and fostering well-being. But beyond biology, there is a spiritual truth-to give love is to remember that you *are* love.

In relationships strained by time or misunderstanding, kindness reintroduces possibility.

It reminds both people that care is still possible, that healing can begin even without perfect words.

In communities divided by difference, kindness becomes common ground-a way of saying,

We may not think alike, but we can still treat each other with humanity.

This shared field of respect is where reconciliation begins.

Living the Circles of Care

Kindness, when practiced consistently, becomes a way of being. It flows outward in widening circles-from the self to the intimate, from the intimate to the collective.

When you extend compassion to yourself, it naturally spills into how you treat others. When you cultivate kindness within your relationships, it shapes the tone of your community.

Each act becomes a thread in the web of connection, weaving resilience into the collective heart.

To live this way is to understand that every interaction carries creative power. You can choose to build or to bruise, to connect or to close.

When you choose kindness, you align with life's natural intelligence-the impulse to nurture, to include, to heal. The world does not soften overnight, but one heart at a time, the tide begins to turn.

And so, through every smile shared, every understanding offered, every wound tended with care, the strength of gentle hands multiplies. Relationships blossom again.

Communities remember their shared heartbeat. And you-quietly, simply, steadily-become part of the living proof that kindness was never weakness; it was always the purest form of strength.

The Hidden Power of Softness

Softness is often mistaken for fragility, but in truth, it is one of the most resilient forces in existence. It bends without breaking, absorbs without losing shape, and moves with grace even when the world grows sharp.

To be soft is to live undefended-not because you are unaware of the world's harshness, but because you trust in something deeper than resistance.

It takes immense courage to remain open when experience has taught you to close.

True softness is not about surrendering your boundaries or diminishing your truth. It is the strength to stand firm in empathy, to let compassion guide you where fear would otherwise build walls.

It is the quiet confidence that understands: vulnerability is not weakness-it is wisdom. It reveals the heart's capacity to love even in uncertainty, to stay present even in discomfort.

The Courage to Stay Open

There are moments in life that ask you to choose between closing off and staying open.

To stay open requires bravery. It means feeling deeply instead of numbing, forgiving instead of hardening, hoping instead of resigning.

This kind of courage does not roar; it breathes. It is found in those who choose tenderness over retaliation, understanding over judgment.

Softness allows you to experience life fully-to let joy in without clinging and pain in without despairing. It teaches you that feeling is not a flaw but a form of truth.

The heart that can hold both ache and awe is unbreakable, because it no longer fears emotion; it trusts it.

This is the essence of living courageously: not in denying the storm, but in learning to dance within it.

Strength in Vulnerability

Vulnerability is the language of softness. It says, *Here I am, as I am.* To speak that language is to walk through life without armor-to let your authenticity be seen, even when the outcome is uncertain.

This is not recklessness; it is reverence for truth. Vulnerability requires strength because it exposes what is real.

It invites connection, compassion, and understanding-but it also risks misunderstanding. The courage lies in showing up anyway.

When you live with softness, you understand that walls may protect, but they also isolate. You trade the illusion of safety for the reality of connection.

You discover that love, creativity, and healing all emerge from openness. Softness makes space for these miracles to happen. It creates an environment where others, too, can lay down their armor and breathe.

The Quiet Resistance of Gentle Souls

In a world that often mistakes hardness for strength, softness becomes a quiet form of resistance.

It says,

I will not let the world harden me.

The gentle soul does not deny pain; it transforms it. Each act of kindness, each choice to respond with compassion instead of cruelty, becomes an act of defiance against apathy.

This is the courage of softness-the refusal to let cynicism win.

Softness does not mean you are unshaken. It means that even when shaken, you do not lose your essence. You continue to care. You continue to believe in goodness.

You continue to reach out, even when it would be easier to withdraw. That persistence is strength in its purest form-steady, grounded, and luminous.

The Tender Art of Self-Compassion

To embody softness outwardly, you must first learn to practice it inwardly.

Courage begins within. It is found in the way you speak to yourself after a mistake, in the patience you offer your own process, in the gentleness with which you hold your growing self.

Self-compassion is not indulgence; it is empowerment. It is the foundation of resilience-the quiet knowing that you can return to tenderness even after the world has been unkind.

When you meet your own struggles with gentleness, you teach your nervous system safety.

You train your heart to trust that it can open again. The inner dialogue shifts from criticism to care, from pressure to patience.

Slowly, softness becomes your default state-not because life is easy, but because you have learned to be kind to yourself through its challenges.

Softness as Presence

To be soft is to be fully present. It is to listen deeply, to observe without judgment, to allow what is without trying to fix it too quickly.

Presence itself is an act of courage-it requires you to stay in the moment rather than escape into distraction or control.

Softness teaches you to trust the unfolding of each breath, to know that not every question needs an immediate answer.

Presence invites peace. When you meet the world softly, time slows. Conversations deepen. Emotions become more navigable.

The space between reaction and response expands, and in that space, understanding grows. You begin to see life not as something to conquer but as something to collaborate with-a dance between your inner rhythm and the world's heartbeat.

Living the Bravery of Softness

Softness as courage is not a single act but a way of living. It is the daily decision to show up with integrity, to lead with empathy, to love without calculation.

It is the way you hold another's hand during their silence, the way you smile at a stranger, the way you forgive yourself for being human.

It is quiet, consistent bravery-the kind that does not demand attention but changes everything it touches.

When you embody this softness, your very presence becomes a sanctuary.

You create ripples of safety around you-places where others can exhale, where honesty feels safe again. This is how gentle hearts heal the world: not through force, but through steadfast tenderness.

And as you walk the spiral of becoming, you will see that softness has always been courage in disguise-the kind that moves mountains not by breaking them, but by wearing them down with patient love.

To be soft is to believe that kindness is powerful enough to last, and that the heart, no matter how many times it opens, always finds its way back to light.

The Quiet Continuum of Love

Love is not a fleeting emotion; it is a living presence that weaves through every moment, even when unseen. To live as proof that love endures is to embody its essence through action, patience, and presence.

It is to understand that love does not disappear when circumstances change or people leave-it transforms, expands, and finds new ways to express itself. True love is not possession but participation; it breathes through the choices we make every day.

Enduring love is not the absence of pain but the ability to hold tenderness within it.

It remembers that loss, disappointment, or distance do not erase the moments that were real. Instead, they invite a deeper kind of love-one that sees beyond outcome and honors the quiet truth of connection.

To live as proof that love endures is to carry that flame forward, even when the world forgets how to keep it lit.

Love as an Ongoing Presence

Love endures not because it resists change, but because it adapts to it.

Like water, it finds new paths when old ones close. It may shift form-from romance to friendship, from longing to gratitude-but its essence remains.

The strength of gentle hands lies in their capacity to continue loving when certainty fades, to keep giving warmth without demand.

When you love beyond attachment, you begin to see love not as something you hold, but as something that holds you.

It becomes the thread connecting you to all living things-the pulse beneath conversation, the space between breaths.

You start to sense love in everything: in the kindness of a stranger, in the stillness of dawn, in the way your heart softens after remembering someone who once mattered deeply. Love is not something you find; it is something you become.

The Practice of Steadfast Care

To live as proof that love endures is to practice care even when no one is watching.

It means choosing kindness over indifference, empathy over avoidance, presence over withdrawal. Love grows in these simple, consistent gestures-the way you listen fully, the way you forgive sincerely, the way you show up even when it is inconvenient.

It is not dramatic but devotional.

In relationships, enduring love manifests as the willingness to keep learning one another, to meet again and again in new seasons of growth.

It honors change instead of fearing it. It creates space for honesty, for vulnerability, for rediscovery. And when parting comes-as it inevitably will in one form or another-this love does not shatter.

It releases with gratitude, trusting that what was real will continue to live in unseen ways.

The Resilience of the Heart

The heart is astonishingly resilient. It breaks and still chooses to love again.

This is the quiet miracle of being human: that even after hurt, we still reach out, still hope, still care. Living as proof that love endures is not about denying the ache of loss; it is about allowing it to shape your compassion.

Pain refines love, stripping it of illusion and revealing its essence-a simple wish for the wellbeing of another.

When you allow the heart to remain open after it has been tested, you carry the legacy of love forward.

You prove that kindness can survive disillusionment, that trust can regrow in the soil of forgiveness, that love's nature is not to end but to evolve.

The endurance of love is not in its permanence but in its ability to renew itself endlessly.

Love as Service to the World

Enduring love extends beyond personal relationships. It becomes a way of serving the world-a quiet offering to the collective heart.

Every time you act with compassion, you are adding to the reservoir of love that sustains humanity.

When you mentor, comfort, protect, or create, you are proving that love still moves through this world, even amid noise and chaos.

In communities, love looks like cooperation over competition, inclusion over isolation. It builds bridges where division once stood.

It listens before it argues, seeks to understand before it corrects. Love endures in every act that nurtures connection.

The gentle hands that hold space for others become instruments of restoration, reminding us that healing is never solitary-it is shared.

The Legacy of Loving Anyway

To love anyway-even after disappointment, even in uncertainty-is one of the greatest expressions of courage.

It is the decision to keep your heart open to life, to believe in the possibility of goodness despite the evidence of imperfection. Living as proof that love endures means carrying that quiet faith into every interaction.

It means being the presence that reminds others it is still safe to care.

Love that endures does not demand recognition. It flows quietly through gestures, words, and silences.

It mends small fractures in the human fabric-a smile that reaches someone on a difficult day, a conversation that restores hope, a moment of forgiveness that breaks the pattern of resentment.

Each act becomes a seed of continuity, keeping love alive where it might have been forgotten.

Becoming the Embodiment of Enduring Love

When love becomes your way of being, you begin to radiate steadiness. People feel safer around you, not because you are perfect, but because you are present.

Your compassion becomes an anchor, your patience a sanctuary. You do not need to speak loudly of love; you live it in the way you move through the world-gently, consistently, and with quiet conviction.

This is the strength of gentle hands: they do not clutch, they cradle. They do not impose, they invite.

They hold without holding back. And through them, love continues-flowing beyond time, beyond circumstance, beyond fear.

To live as proof that love endures is to remember that every small act of care ripples into eternity, carrying light into places that have forgotten it.

And as you walk through life with this understanding, you realize something simple yet profound: love does not need to be proven by words or grand gestures.

Your presence, your patience, your unwavering kindness-they are all the proof the world needs.

Through you, love endures, quietly but infinitely, reminding humanity of what it was always meant to be.